Praise for
If You Could Talk to an *Angel*

"Tears of sadness rolled down my face when I asked Margaret a question that had been troubling me. However, tears of complete joy flooded my body when I got the answer. This book is pure and powerful and so very comforting. When something moves me to my core, I call it 'big medicine.' Gerry Gavin's book If You Could Talk to an Angel, *is just that: big, soul medicine. Cherish it and pass it on—for it is a gift."*

— **Kris Carr,** *New York Times* best-selling author of
Crazy Sexy Juice and *Crazy Sexy Kitchen*

"If You Could Talk to an Angel is a special book that not only helped me to understand the deeper questions about life—and made me think— but also touched my soul!"

— **John Holland,** medium, spiritual teacher, and best-selling author
of *The Spirit Whisperer: Chronicles of a Medium*

"If You Could Talk to an Angel is an inspiring and compelling read. The tenderhearted messages bring celestial guidance on countless issues from personal purpose and relationships to learning how to connect with your own guardian angel. Don't miss this comprehensive guide to finding your soul's perspective on love, compassion, and forgiveness—and on creating a wonderful and fulfilling life now!"

— **Sandra Anne Taylor,** *New York Times* best-selling author of
Your Quantum Breakthrough Code

"As a Note from the Universe once said, everyone should be using all of their angels—and Gerry's Margaret shows exactly why. Their deep love and profound insights into life and its mechanics offer truths that can set us all free from limiting beliefs and undesirable patterns of manifestation. Reading Margaret is like bringing cool water to parched lips."

— **Mike Dooley,** *New York Times* best-selling author of *Infinite Possibilities*
and *The Top Ten Things Dead People Want to Tell YOU*

"If you're a fan of the Abraham-Hicks material, then you're going to love If You Could Talk to an Angel. *Full of answers to the deepest questions that we all have, and presented in a simple yet profound manner, this book will bring you a deep sense of peace, contentment, and a knowing that all is well!"*

— **Nick Ortner,** *New York Times* best-selling author, producer,
and CEO of The Tapping Solution, LLC

"When I read If You Could Talk to an Angel, *it just brought the biggest smile to my face. One of the first spiritual materials I was attracted to as a teenager was the work of Abraham-Hicks, and this book instantly reminded me of how much I love this style of writing and sharing of information. I love the way this book is presented, especially in the way it shares the answers to so many things many of us often contemplate at our core. Gerry and Margaret clearly care about their audience, and it comes through in this book. This is the kind of book you can just open up daily to a random page, and receive profound wisdom from."*

— **Emmanuel Dagher,** humanitarian, transformation specialist, and author of *Easy Breezy Prosperity*

"Even though some of us feel connected with the other side, there is always a deeper perspective that comes through the angelic truth in Margaret's messages. If You Could Talk to an Angel *rings with that deeper truth. Today I am a better husband, father, friend, and human being because of this new beautiful book. Thank you, Gerry and Margaret, for making a better me."*

— **James John,** spiritual counselor, messenger, author of *How to Love Myself and Others*, and founder of *LAF: Love Appreciate Forgive,* www.LivingLAF.com

"Just as Gerry brings Margaret's voice to the world, her words—along with Gerry's inspirational story—moved me personally to expand my work in helping messengers to trust their wisdom and bring it to life on the page and in the world. This book answers so many important questions while giving us the courage to know that everyone's words—especially their questions—really matter!"

— **Christine Kloser,** "The Transformation Catalyst" and award-winning author of *Pebbles in the Pond: Transforming the World One Person at a Time*

"Never in the history of this planet have we had so much access to spirit and answers we've been yearning for our entire lives. Margaret shares heartfelt guidance and timeless wisdom that both inspires and empowers those who connect with her."

— **Jennifer Kass,** spiritual mentor, writer, and speaker

If You Could
Talk to an
Angel

ALSO BY GERRY GAVIN

Books

*Messages from Margaret: Down-to-Earth
Angelic Advice for the World . . . and You**

CDs/DVDs

Angels & Shamans (audio workshop on CD or MP3)

Drum Music for the Shamanic Journey or Shamanic Tapping (MP3)

*Available from Hay House

Please visit:

Hay House USA: www.hayhouse.com®
Hay House Australia: www.hayhouse.com.au
Hay House UK: www.hayhouse.co.uk
Hay House South Africa: www.hayhouse.co.za
Hay House India: www.hayhouse.co.in

If You Could Talk to an Angel

Angelic Answers to Your Questions on Life, Love, Purpose, and More

GERRY GAVIN

HAY HOUSE, INC.
Carlsbad, California • New York City
London • Sydney • Johannesburg
Vancouver • Hong Kong • New Delhi

Published and distributed in the United States by: Hay House, Inc.: www
.hayhouse.com® • **Published and distributed in Australia by:** Hay House Australia Pty. Ltd.: www.hayhouse.com.au • **Published and distributed in the United
Kingdom by:** Hay House UK, Ltd.: www.hayhouse.co.uk • **Published and distributed in the Republic of South Africa by:** Hay House SA (Pty), Ltd.: www.hayhouse
.co.za • **Distributed in Canada by:** Raincoast Books: www.raincoast.com • **Published in India by:** Hay House Publishers India: www.hayhouse.co.in

Project editor: Nicolette Salamanca Young
Cover design: Gaelyn Larrick • *Interior design:* Nick C. Welch

Library of Congress Cataloging-in-Publication Data

Names: Gavin, Gerry, date.
Title: If you could talk to an angel : angelic answers to your questions on
   life, love, purpose, and more / Gerry Gavin.
Description: Carlsbad : Hay House, Inc., 2016.
Identifiers: LCCN 2015037306 | ISBN 9781401947507 (tradepaper : alk. paper)
Subjects: LCSH: Angels. | Spiritual life.
Classification: LCC BF1999 .G3874 2016 | DDC 202/.15--dc23 LC record available
   at http://lccn.loc.gov/2015037306

ISBN: 978-1-4019-4750-7

10 9 8 7 6 5 4 3 2 1
1st edition, February 2016

Printed in the United States of America

To Reid Tracy.
Thank you for urging me
to give Margaret a voice!

CONTENTS

INTRODUCTION

My journey to becoming a published author has been a truly amazing experience! And the story of how this book came to be is direct proof of that statement. I'd been drafting a proposal for my second book, trying to draw together the two areas that I'm blessed to work with every day—shamanism and communicating with angels. But for some reason the ideas weren't flowing, and it was a struggle to develop even a rough chapter outline. Frustrated, I reached out for some assistance from my angel, Margaret.

Now, I don't use the word *angel* figuratively to mean Margaret is a wonderful person—she is an actual angel. I have been privileged to be channeling her for nearly 25 years, a sort of "celestial pen pal" who offers personal guidance as well as insight into the world. (You can find the full story of how we met in my first book, *Messages from Margaret*. Go to www.gerrygavin.com to download the first chapter for free.) After so many years of delivering Margaret's amazing and inspirational messages to people all over the world—and seeing the incredible results this has on their lives—I felt that she was exactly who I needed to speak to about my writer's block.

Margaret quickly pointed out that the reason I was having such a hard time was that I was trying to create something other than what my soul truly desired to write. She then asked if she could please construct a new book proposal along with a personal letter from her to the CEO of Hay House, Reid Tracy!

Although this might seem like a rather unusual request, it was Reid who made the decision to take a chance on publishing my first book. He was also the one who urged me to "give a voice" to her, which led to Margaret speaking live (through me) to international callers every week on HayHouseRadio.com. So when I told him that I had a personal letter and book proposal for him from an angel, he was not taken aback one bit.

Margaret asked: *What if you could sit down in your home with an angel and had the chance to ask any question about life that you most wanted answered? What questions would you love to ask an angelic being that has the ability to see the "big picture"?* She came up with the title *If You Could Talk to an Angel,* and proposed that the content be composed of her answers to mankind's burning questions, submitted by fans from around the world.

Reid loved the idea, but took it a step further. He felt that if we reached out to some of the world's most prominent new-thought writers—the people on the cutting edge of all things related to the mind, body, and spirit—they would shed light on even more expansive topics. So that is exactly what you will find in these pages, as 20 best-selling authors excitedly jumped on board to be part of the book and set the tone for the incredible quality of questions! (If you would like to learn more about the wonderful authors who have contributed questions, their particular names are set in bold text to signify that their full bios can be found in the back of this book.)

Hundreds upon hundreds of people responded to our request for questions. We were so pleased to see numerous countries on many different continents, as well as a wide variety of professions, represented. We received questions from a forensic scientist, a neuroscientist, energy healers, teachers, an adult-film actress and activist, musicians, mothers, and more. Margaret and I struggled with the task of how to select the ones to answer. All were, to say the least, amazing! Some of the answers were so deeply personal that we decided to answer those through direct communication rather than within these pages. We also selected a few to answer through the *Messages from Margaret* online radio show, my website blog, or Facebook posts. Finally, after weeks of review and deliberation, Margaret and I were able to narrow down 33 questions to run alongside the 20 author questions. I trust that you will find them representative of some of mankind's most pressing questions about life, and hope that you thereby find the answers to some of your own. If not, I urge you to contact us with your question through my website or Facebook page at facebook.com/messagesfrommargaret.

All of the chapters that follow are Margaret's direct words, which she channeled through me. They offer wonderful original insights into many topics that I had never truly understood before. One of Margaret's greatest strengths is her ability to explain complicated concepts in such a "down-to-earth" manner that you find yourself suddenly feeling much smarter than you ever imagined yourself to be and feeling like you've somehow "remembered" something real and true. Some of her explanations are so simple that you will be amazed that you did not already understand them. Others are detailed in easy-to-understand explanations. Some might even be considered controversial; all are deeply insightful.

Clearly this book would not have been possible without the questions that were submitted by these wonderful authors and seekers. I was so touched by the honesty and vulnerability of the questions and the personal stories submitted. This book gives us a wonderful glimpse into just how alike we all are. Whether we are the author or the reader, we are all in our own way the teacher and the student, and we are so very lucky to have each other on this journey!

With deepest thanks and love,
Gerry Gavin

ALL ABOUT THE UNIVERSE

Energy, Angels, and You

> *"When you are here in your earthly existence . . .*
> *it is hard for you to imagine the enormous*
> *energy that is your soul."*

Hello, my dear ones, and welcome! I am so happy to have this opportunity to speak to you, and I hope to answer your most burning questions about life in ways that will help you better celebrate it.

I cannot emphasize enough how important your questions are. Everything around you—all of the inventions, conveniences, theories, and beliefs that you have today—started with a question that someone once asked. Questions are at the very core of the creative process; not only do they cause humans to look more deeply into something, but also they create energy that manifests solutions to those very concerns!

I want to thank all of those who asked the questions that helped create this book. Thank you, readers and radio listeners from all over the world. You may not realize it, but the questions that you ask every day actually manifest the answers to those questions—and one of those manifestations is this book that you are reading.

To the many authors, teachers, and healers who also invested your trust in me, I offer you the most sincere of thanks. You asked questions that were both profound and helpful, and many of you shared deeply personal anecdotes of your own angelic experiences as well. I hope that the answers within will enable you to take your work to greater levels of service and success!

Together, you did a wonderful job of touching upon many of life's great mysteries, which come up so often—both in the conversations that I have with you all through Gerry as well as the questions that you all often think to yourselves.

One of the most often asked has to do with the nature of your true existence, and I want to begin this book with a heartfelt story and question from *Carina Rubin,* a tarot, angel, and manifestation coach from Mexico City. She writes:

> *When I was a teenager, I believed in absolutely nothing. I thought we were born, we lived, and we died—and that was it. That was a very dark time in my life because I couldn't find a purpose in life, and so I couldn't find a reason to live. I kept asking myself: "What's the purpose of life?" Finally, the universe started showing me there is so much more than this physical existence. Today I see that this life is just a tiny little part of the whole soul experience, and a soul is just a tiny little part of this whole universe. So now my original question has expanded: "What's the purpose of the soul experience, and what's the purpose of the existence of the universe?"*

This question has been on the minds of men and women through innumerable centuries. To answer this question I would ask you to imagine for a moment that your essence—the true essence of who you are—is only two steps away from the Creator of all things in the process of creation. Because, in fact, that is the case!

In the beginning there was only the Creator, and the Creator was a being of perfect light and love. The Creator desired to expand that light and love and share it—but in order to expand something you need to have an opposing energy. Therefore, to expand the light, the Creator would need to create darkness. The energy of the

Creator was drawn into a ball of light so dense and powerful that it exploded. In doing so, it created light matter and spaces between the light, which you have come to know as dark matter. This event has even been named in science: the "big bang."

Immediately following the creation of dark matter, there came into existence the energetic beings you now know as *angels*. They were very close to and were connected to the essence of the Creator, but were at the same time independent beings of darkness and of light. Angels themselves expanded their energy and, in unison with the Creator, formed another category of energetic being you have come to know as *souls*. Yes—this is who you are! The Creator then remained and to this day remains interconnected with the energy of all things that were created from that original "big bang." Its consciousness is aware of, and interacts with, all aspects of creation from the most complex universal galaxies to the smallest microbial structures. And everything else in the universe, all other matter that you know of and do not yet know of, stems from these three energetic forms working in unison.

From there, the expansion of the universe was totally and completely dependent on you. At the time of your creation, you were given the option of either remaining a being of pure light, existing in a state of total bliss and love and harmony, or learning about the nature of those things that are not from your same energy. By placing your energy into containers of dense physical matter, the Creator, the angels, and you could all experience what it's like to *be* that creation! Furthermore, you could then use these forms to *create new life* that would grow and learn from and teach the other forms that you inhabited. These physical forms would also have an ability called *thought* that would allow you to call and manipulate particles of energy and thereby affect the creation of matter. In this way, you would allow all things in the universe to expand and evolve to new life forms.

You were given this choice: live forever in a state of total bliss in the expanded loving energy of the Creator or experience the full spectrum of everything that had been created. The latter choice could bring pain, sadness, and loneliness; no knowledge of who you truly were; and even physical death. But it would also bring experiences of love, happiness, and beauty in ever-expanding forms. So as souls you took on this amazing challenge to allow the universe its incredible and constant expansion!

In short, the purpose of the soul experience and the purpose of the universe are one and the same: the universe is constantly expanding by the energy that you as souls invest in all forms of physical matter. You as souls place small pieces of yourselves, known as your *consciousness,* in physical containers that allow you to experience the full spectrum of creation—the darkness and the light. Doing so expands the number of potential possibilities to an endless degree and, in turn, expands the universe.

Truly, that is something that we angels admire about you as souls. When we were created, we were given dominion over creating the darkness and the light and all of the potential possibilities of those creations. But you were created only of the light and given the choice as to what you would like to experience. The very symbolic biblical story of Adam and Eve alludes to the genesis of the path of the souls. They/you were created in total bliss and then given the choice of staying in that state or taking from the "tree of knowledge." That symbolic tree would give you the ability to know of everything that had been created, but once you chose the fruit of that tree, there would be no turning back.

≫

So that, dear ones, is why you decided to allow yourself to become aware of the existence of all different types of energies through all types of physical forms. When you are here in your earthly existence, I know it is hard for you to imagine the enormous energy that is your soul. So many of you see your souls as separate spiritual beings that enter your bodies, suffer through life, die, and may potentially suffer through the afterlife based on your actions during your life! Indeed, *Marilyn Enness,* a retired elementary school teacher from Stanton, Michigan, seems to understand that there is more to your soul than this. She wondered:

In the physical realm we have many, many longings. Do we have longings in the spirit realm? Do we perhaps long to come to Earth?

It is true that much of what you desire in the physical realm has its roots in the soul realm. But when you are in this realm, in your full soul form, the energy of love is all encompassing and the response to a desire is instantaneous. You have the ability to create and place yourself in any experience that you might wish, almost like a movie in which you could not only see but also feel all the emotions and wonderful sensations. If you were to imagine the most sophisticated virtual reality system that you could develop on earth, then multiply that potential by one million, it would not come close to the bliss that you feel at your soul state.

You have an enormous and ever-expanding amount of energy in your pure soul state right now, which many of you also refer to as your *higher self.* Your soul is the essence of your consciousness, which is the energy that empowers your physical body. Your higher self exists apart from, but connected to, all of your human forms and can see you at all times in your different lifetimes. It is as though your soul is this masterful director, able to cast part of itself (individual consciousness) into all of these different roles/incarnations. Information from these experiences is shared with your fellow souls to determine what types of future physical incarnations and experiences you would like to create together. You watch the physical realm from your control booth and yet still are able to interact with other souls, angels, and the Creator because the energy of your higher self is so profound. And everywhere—everywhere—there is joy!

Remember, however, that it is your allowing yourself to experience and accumulate the understanding of joy and sadness and ultimately love and fear in the physical plane that allows you to create pure bliss at the soul level. The more you understand the opposite of joy, the more profound the experience of joy becomes!

Many of you have come to call this place where your soul resides between the birth and death of a physical incarnation, "heaven." In many stories, heaven is portrayed as a place or a state where there is no worry, no strife, no hunger, no prejudice, and no money worries; everyone simply loves one another. This is very accurate to your existence as your higher self, and as a physical being you continually get energetic hits about who you truly are as a soul. In fact, part of your physical journey is trying to remember or reconnect with your true soul state. Many times you enlist the help of other seekers who join together in spiritual groups to try to understand the struggles of life and the nature of the afterlife.

One of the things many are curious about—because you can feel our constant presence—is the existence of angels. In fact, in numerous well-respected national polls, over 70 percent of people from many different religions said they believed in angels, while more than 50 percent indicated they had a personal "angelic experience."

Medical intuitive **Mona Lisa Schulz, M.D., Ph.D.**, author of *The Intuitive Advisor* and co-author with Louise Hay of *All Is Well*, is a master at blending explanations of the worlds of science and energy. She very eloquently brought the question to the table of how so many diverse religions share these beliefs:

The world is filled with different religions, each with different understandings and points of view of what angels are, where they live, and how they communicate to us—how do we understand this? How can we reconcile this? Do you have a way of explaining angels that every religion and spirituality can relate to?

One common thread in religions worldwide is that they *all* believe in the existence of angels. We are the one commonality in a world of differences, and in almost all of those religions we serve as the messengers of the Creator.

In *Messages from Margaret,* I spoke about the creation of religions. In the earliest days, mankind would align itself with whatever image of a god would seem to be responding to their desires for power and abundance. A tribe no longer had to be physically strong or large in numbers if they could show that they had a god who had helped them to rise to some form of greatness. And when one man-created deity would let them down, people would create another.

It was at that time that the Creator sent angels to act in our role as messenger. We appeared to many of the major nations with the express purpose of sharing the message that everyone is equally loved, and equally deserving of greatness, in the eyes of the Creator. In every case, we found wonderful human messengers, who became known as prophets, to understand and carry these messages to their tribes. In some cases, the same angels would speak to different tribes, in order to show them that this message was for everyone. We spoke in each tongue and dialect. We honored each cultural difference so that there would be no resistance. In all cases the message was to love one another equally.

Every religion and culture had a different word for us, but all saw us as the messengers for the divine. Gabriel came to announce the birth of Jesus, and he appeared to Muhammad to help him craft the Koran. Michael is regarded as a protector of the peoples of Israel. The angel Moroni led John Smith to the golden plates, which became the Book of Mormon. We are the "Concourse on High" to the Baha'i faith and *fravashi* to the Zoroastrian religion. Hindus speak of the presence of *devas,* while the ancient Greeks spoke of *aggelos,* "messengers," from which the name *angel* derives. The Romans called us *genii,* meaning guardian angels.

Although we made our presence known to every religion and culture, somehow, still, men proclaimed that their religion or people were the preferred one! In appearing to all cultures, our purpose was to show that the Creator equally loved and created all. It was the human leaders of the different groups and fledgling religions that created the dogma to set their faith apart from others. They tried to limit those who could speak to the angels, saying only the original prophets or some ordained holy person was able to do so.

Our message has been constant and unrelenting. Our message is straight from the Creator, and that message is love! Just as you love your family, so too must you love the family of man. Just as you love your son or daughter, know that other people in other cultures love their son and daughter. Just as you love your mother and father, know that it is the same for others around the world. Just as you love to laugh and feel joy, so is it the same in every culture of the world. And as you believe in the existence of angels, so do they—and all of you have guardians, many of them the same as those in other cultures. In many cases, you may have even incarnated into a simultaneous life in a culture for which you do not have much feelings of love right now.

And we angels are, again, speaking through so many regular people who share the same universal message: love one another!

∽

More than just messengers of the Creator, angels have been imagined by humans in many ways, from nurturing to destructive, in all forms of artistic likenesses. Along with these varying images, differing theories came forth as to what exactly an angel is. There seems to be much confusion between angels and other spiritual forms. In this vein, **Anita Moorjani**, world-renowned motivational speaker and *New York Times* best-selling author of *Dying to Be Me*, asked:

> *I feel guided all the time, particularly after my near-death experience. Most of the time, I can identify the guidance as coming from some of my deceased loved ones. So, Margaret, would you say that angels and deceased loved ones are the same? In other words, have my loved ones become angels after crossing over?*

I thank you so very much for this question, Anita, because it is one of the most misunderstood concepts about our differing energetic forms. An understanding of the nature of angels, spirit guides, and ancestors that have crossed over has eluded mankind for centuries. I hope this answer clarifies the nature of all these spiritual energies and how we interact with each other as well as those of you who are currently incarnated in a physical form.

Many believe that angels were once physical beings, such as humans who lived a good life and then passed on. However, while angels have the ability to project the illusion of a physical form, we are not and have never been physical beings. When you see us in a physical form, it is rather like a hologram, a projection of energy that manipulates light and shadow to cause you to see a physical form. We are an entirely different energetic form than your ancestors that have crossed back to their soul state. But these ancestors can, and generally do, help those whom they have left behind. So when you perceive energy that feels extremely similar to someone with whom you have shared a lifetime, you are indeed feeling the influence of their energy, which has now returned to the state of their higher self.

Some souls learn to work beyond the illusions of their physicality and decide to incarnate less frequently, or stay within the state of their higher self and turn their purpose toward helping incarnating souls. They have achieved an advanced level of understanding, and focus love and compassion. These souls are referred to as *spirit guides* or *saints*. Spirit guides in their physical form were often known as prophets and were regarded as having a direct connection to the Creator or the angelic realm, sharing messages for the purpose of helping all of mankind. Their ability to access their higher self while still in human form means that they are sometimes able to "see" things beyond the limits of space and time—and for this reason they might be credited with prophecy.

Ancestors are all the other souls, those that leave their physical form behind and return to their higher self. All of them help other souls on the physical realm in any way possible. But one thing holds common for all angels, guides, and ancestors: *We cannot interfere with your free will and cannot offer help when it is not requested by you or someone asking for help on your behalf!* We can only assist when there is a loving or compassionate request for help.

Although the three levels of spiritual energy (the Creator, angels, then souls) each vibrate at different frequencies, it is very important to understand that just because something is vibrating at a "higher" frequency, that does not mean it is somehow better or more evolved. Angels do not see themselves as better than souls, and the Creator does not see himself/herself as being any greater than souls or angels. To do this would be like thinking that your leg was better than your arm, your brain better than your skin. Each part of the body has its own intrinsic importance and works in unison with the others! To think that one part is more important is a judgment, and there is no judgment in the spiritual plane. There is only experience, and all experience is perceived by your higher selves in a loving, compassionate, and grateful manner.

∞

Personal-growth speaker **Noah St. John** was very surprised one day when he received a Facebook message from Gerry saying that he not only had earthly fans but also angelic fans! Gerry told Noah that his teachings are very angelically inspired and that, like him, angels see the questions you ask yourself as key to the experiences you are creating.

While this book is the result of people asking questions of an angel, Noah explores the concept of your internal and external questions in his best-selling book, *Afformations®: The Miracle of Positive Self-Talk*. Noah uses a play on the word *affirmation,* which is a positive statement of what you want in your life; in contrast, an Afformation is a *question*. It is a way to reframe a problem as a question that is yet to be answered, while being sure to ask yourself only *empowering* questions.

For example, if you are going through financial difficulty, your mind may already be inundated with disempowering questions like "How did I get into this mess?" or "Why is there always more month than money?" Negative phrasing such as this leads your brain to find negative answers for them, for that is what the brain does. Afformations are a very good tool to lift your vibration and change your energy. If you instead ask yourself empowering questions like "Why is it so easy for me to make more money?" the brain goes off on a search to prove why it is actually simple to bring forth the energy of past successes. You can often hear me on the *Messages from Margaret* radio program advising callers to change their mind-set in just this way.

Noah is a down-to-earth man who always seeks to understand the inner workings of everything. Naturally, his question for me was as profound as it was simple. He asked:

What is it like to be an angel?

I believe many humans must see the work of angels as almost tedious—running around all over the planet and being asked to help people with everything from serious health concerns to finding a parking spot. (We love doing both!) In truth, I believe that we have an amazing life because we have the opportunity to assist the Creator and all the souls of the universe in a principle as easy as ABC: "Always Be Creating!" We possess the ability to create with thought, thus assisting the Creator and souls in creating the framework for all of creation.

We have no need for rest; so you could say that we are on duty 24/7! (Our "days," however, are not encumbered by the confines of space and time; such things are actually physical creations.) As an extension of the Creator, every angel possesses an individual skill set that is part of the consciousness of the Creator—as do you. We assist souls through the use of our skill sets to achieve the expansion of light, love, and compassion throughout the universe.

Angels are basically the "engineers" of the thought universe. We create energetic frameworks from thoughts that you think, as well as from the thoughts of the Creator. When souls desire to manifest something into physical reality, we figure out how to create the energetic framework that will allow that thought to be made physical.

The Creator works from a much higher point of view; he/she asks us to create frameworks to allow for love, compassion, and understanding to have new ways to be communicated to all creatures throughout the universe in an energetic language that all will understand. Sometimes we are able to create that structure almost immediately; sometimes it may take "years" for the reality of this thought structure to be accepted by mankind. Social issues, such as civil rights and sexual equality, take generations for souls to accept the energetic framework we design; this is because you always have free will to accept or reject the framework. Sometimes acceptance will take a full evolution of a species. But if it is in the interest of the expansion of love, peace, compassion, and joy, we will keep reimagining that framework! This is one of our ongoing challenges.

I am one of those angels whose skill set is that of communication, and this is why you, much to my joy, find me here, hopefully answering your questions to the degree that it will increase your level of peace, love, compassion, and understanding of your fellow humans. In fact, the gender that you perceive for angels is based on the vibration of the task or specialty that we offer. For example, you perceive me, as a communicator, as feminine and Michael, as a protector, as masculine because that is the best vibration to put forth the energy of the roles we play in your assistance. In truth, we have no specific gender but rather possess the energy of both, just as you do in your soul state.

Angels are beings of complete love and compassion, even those who are angels of the dark matter—for all of the energy of dark matter is there to support the energy of the light and to create a basis for comparison. It is a misconception to think that an angel of darkness is an evil being. The energy of dark matter is often the exact opposite of the experience of light matter; in essence, creating what some of you have come to call the yin and yang of life. Many people discover the energy of their light by first exploring their shadow self, or by experiencing what has been described as the "dark night of the soul." Different angels create from the light and the darkness, so when experiences make you feel removed from the light, it is only because you have *chosen* to experience something in this manner, so that you can find the light behind it!

In our eyes, you souls are amazing; we are enamored of your courageousness in taking on these life forms, navigating and growing through experiences of light and darkness, all the while experiencing amnesia for a period—sometimes an entire lifetime—as to the depth of who you really are. So we are overjoyed to do anything that you might ask of us, whether it's help with a task or help to remember the essence of your being!

As angels, we live an entirely blissful existence. Never experiencing the pain of disappointment or judging something else as being better than, we see everything as just perfect. We interact with each other, your higher selves, and the Creator, and together we continually work to expand the universe.

Imagine the bliss you would experience as a human being if you never had to worry about bills or your health: you love your job and everyone loves you and you love everyone else! Imagine if every day were continually better than the day before. There is a wonderful line from your movie *Apollo 13* about the moon voyage: "Failure is not an option!" Now imagine living this phrase every day; that is completely true for us angels as well as for you in your soul state.

That is what it is like to be an angel: to know nothing but success and unencumbered love and bliss. All in all, not a bad existence. Or as you would say, Noah—why is it so easy to be an angel!

~

While you now know what we do in our daily life as angels, *Mandi Morrissey,* a human-resources professional from Minneapolis, Minnesota, wanted more information about the specific details. She wondered:

> *I understand that time is not linear to angels, but how do they spend their time when they are not with us? Do they have hobbies, pets, and families, or do they just pass time with each other? Are new angels ever "born"?*

Angels love to share in the experiences of souls. You might say that we live vicariously through you. All of your experiences upload to the collective soul, which is the collective consciousness of all of your higher selves. Since all angels are interconnected to those souls, it allows us to partake in the energetic feelings that different soul experiences create.

As energetic beings, we create tones from our vibrations, which one might hear as music or a celestial "voice." You may have heard that angels sing the praises of the Creator. What is actually being referred to is the beautiful tonal frequency of our vibration and how it harmonizes with the vibration of the Creator. You in turn express similar internal vibrations in the tones and music you create, both with your human voices and the instruments you have invented.

We do not have pets in what you refer to as heaven—but we constantly interact with the energy of animals on all planets. We also don't have families in the way that you think of the word. Our "children," if you will, would be you in your soul state, since we were involved in creating you.

Everything that exists was created at the time of the big bang, so there are no "new" angels to speak of. However, there are times that we will reach a level of energetic growth and complexity, and our energy will split and divide into more than one energy form. To explain this I would like to use the example of a tree. Rather than expanding its energy by growing larger and larger into the sky, this tree instead drops acorns, which contain the essence of the tree, around itself. Those acorns are interconnected to the original consciousness of its maker, and allow the tree to expand its energy into a form that is just like its original self. If you were to dig up the tree that sprouted from this acorn and move it to another location, it would be a part of new surroundings and experiences while still being an extension of that original tree.

Like you, we are always seeking ways to expand our energy. As you expand your energy through the frameworks that we angels create, it expands ours as well! It is much like your stock market: when a stock grows to a certain level, it is split into shares that are smaller and more affordable so that more people can participate in its growth potential of abundance and subsequent joy. You do the same as a soul.

❧

Part of my work with Gerry is to help all of you to see that, in contrast to what most of you learned about life, "Life was not meant to be hard!" You so often perceive life as a series of challenges or hurdles that you have to get over; the more difficult the hurdles that you encounter, the more difficult you expect your future hurdles to be.

Part of the message that I offer, both in this book and through Gerry in readings and other ways, is that if you reframe your thinking, then you will begin to see that the world is conspiring in your favor! To illustrate this thought, I would like to share something that came up in a reading with a young woman who was a very accomplished track star at her school. She was struggling with the pole vault; specifically she was able to clear eight and a half feet, but she could not seem to get to nine. She'd been unable to reach this goal for four years, and it was affecting her status on the team.

I pointed out to her that since nine feet seemed like an impossible task, then it shouldn't be her goal. I asked her to stand up and lift her left leg six inches from the ground. She did so, and when I asked her if it had been difficult for her, she said, "No, that was very easy!" I then told her that she should stop thinking about trying to pole-vault nine feet; instead, she should remember how easy it was to pick up her foot and realize that she only had to jump six inches higher than she always did! You can accomplish so much by simply reframing your thoughts—and, sometimes, asking for a little help from an angelic "specialist."

On the topic of angels and their specialties, it is important to note that angels do not necessarily work alone. Sometimes we work as a team, as was the case with the assistance provided to **Sandra Anne Taylor,** who is an international speaker, counselor, and the *New York Times* best-selling author of *Your Quantum Breakthrough Code.* Sandra was kind enough to share her story of angelic intervention with you here:

> I have walked with the angels throughout my life, but they really came to my assistance when my husband and I were adopting our two children. I had been pursuing all options, domestic and foreign, but I was confused about which avenue to follow. The only thing my husband and I were sure of was that we wanted to adopt older children because kids over the age of eight were usually disregarded due to their age.
>
> One night as I was falling asleep, I asked Raphael, the angel of love and travel, for help. That night I had a dream where I was clearly told, "Go to St. Petersburg." So I started looking for agencies that worked with orphanages in St. Petersburg, Russia, but I seemed to have no luck. Still, I kept asking for help.
>
> One afternoon, after hitting yet another roadblock, I called out, "Tell me what I need to do!" Within a few minutes of that little outburst, I received a phone call from a friend telling me about a foreign-adoption meeting taking place that evening about an hour away from my home. I immediately decided to go, but just a few

hours before the meeting was to start, a huge snowstorm rolled in. I then got another call from my friend telling me it was to be a meeting of women adopting infants from South America. That information, along with the snow, made me think that perhaps I shouldn't bother going. But as soon as I had that thought, I clearly heard, "Go to the meeting." And when the message is that clear, I listen.

So there I was, driving through the blinding snow, thinking I was crazy, but I kept plowing through. When I got to the meeting, the ladies sat in a circle and told their stories. I was frustrated that none of their information seemed to apply to me until I happened to look at the woman next to me. She was holding an adoption magazine that I'd never heard of, and the entire issue was devoted to Russian adoption! On the back cover of the magazine was an ad for an agency that worked with an orphanage in St. Petersburg placing older children. In fact, the feature article was about a woman who adopted an older child from St. Petersburg, precisely the experience I was looking for!

My husband and I ended up using that very agency and orphanage to find the two wonderful children we adopted: our daughter, Vica, then 12 years old, and our son, Jenyaa, then 11 years old. But providence and assistance didn't stop with the message that I go to that meeting! There were so many times where Raphael and other spirit friends came through to help, even up to our final days in Russia, clearing stuck paperwork, moving the process forward, and even finding my lost passport, without which we would not have been able to complete the adoption.

We brought our children home on Christmas Eve, and we knew we loved each other before we could even speak the same language! I know without a doubt that these children were destined to be with us. And I'm certain that Raphael, who is also the angel of miracles and family connections, played an undeniable part in bringing us together!

Sandra is clearly a believer in the amazing abilities that angels have to create miracles in your lives when you empower them to do so! Her question for me was:

I know that we have at least one "guardian angel" that stays with us for life, but do they remain with us for lifetime after lifetime? (This makes me wonder if Margaret is—and has been—your personal guardian angel all along!)

Before answering your question, dear one, I want to first speak to you for a moment about your amazing situation and how you allowed yourself to fall into the pathway of miracles by trusting your intuition. When you seek—and call upon us for help—we do everything in our power to bring to you the situations that would help inspire the visions of what you are creating. But what helps us so much is when you stay unwaveringly focused on that thought, which is what you did when you thought to adopt.

Then you listened for the answer. You listened for the quiet voice inside that puts ideas into your head, ways for you to move in the direction that you desired. Those were angelic voices and, just as you came to be able to hear them, so too can everyone hear. But it does take a little bit of focus and the firm belief that you are connected to a source of knowledge beyond your five senses. And this brings us to your question on how such a connection between angels and humankind takes place.

Angels were very instrumental in your creation, just as earth beings are directly involved with the creation of their children. Each angel assists the Creator in the manifestation of a being of soul energy, and in doing so shares part of its energy within the energetic structure of that soul. This is the actual nature of what you have come to call DNA. It begins with the energetic imprint of the Creator, then the energetic imprint of the angel who assisted in the creation of a soul, and then the soul passes on that imprint to the physical beings it manifests.

So when we speak of your "guardian angel," we are actually speaking of the angel who aided in your soul's creation, as that angel is forever connected to that soul in all of its forms of incarnation. (Your guardian angel will also have aided in the creation of other souls, and these souls form your "soul group.") So yes, dear one, I have been Gerry's guardian throughout all of his lifetimes and in all of his life forms. But Gerry has not developed the ability to speak with me in the manner that we communicate today in every lifetime.

While your personal guardian angel has been with you through all of time, you also attract to you other angels that assist you in various tasks you seek to perform. All angels have been imbued with certain creative skills that we use to create frameworks to assist a soul. In my specialty as a communicator, I am skilled in finding ways to "translate" different complicated concepts into easily understood language. Other angels have other skills in numerous different areas, such as geometric design, healing, and music (which is also referred to spiritually as "frequency modulation and harmony"). We always ask each other for help, as there is no ego involved in being an angel. The most important thing is finding creative suggestions to successfully help you.

For example, when you sought to find the perfect children to adopt, you put forth a certain concept into the universe. Then a team of angels began to work on your request. Your energetic frequency and the energetic frequency of children all over the world were matched up. Then this angelic team delved deeper into the qualifications of the potential matches in order to discover the best possible combination for you in terms of personality, geographic location, and possibility of navigating the rules and regulations of adoption. Finally, the angels who specialize in soul-level "negotiation" spoke to the higher selves of those who would stand in the way of the adoption and helped them understand that it really was for the better good. However, it was the singular clarity of your focus that allowed your guardian angel to assemble this wonderful team to in turn shape this wonderful event.

~

Mandi Morrissey wondered if there are ever exceptions to the rule that your guardian angel sticks with you from lifetime to lifetime. She asked:

Do angels ever leave us (as humans) if we make a decision that they don't like? There are humans with the worst intentions who make bad decisions and harm others; do they still have angels with them?

We never leave our connection to you as humans because we never leave you as a higher self. There is no action that you could take that would cause us to abandon you, because we place no judgment on your actions. Even the worst decisions, with the worst human motivations, can propel other souls to amazing heights of energetic growth. Everything human is only temporary to your soul and as such all experiences lead to growth—as hard as that might be for you to believe!

∽

Isn't it amazing that each of you has an angel that is so deeply energetically connected, always aware of your desires and wishing so much to help you achieve joy? You might wonder, then, why it seems so difficult for many to open up to angelic communication. This connection was on the mind of *Laura Botsford,* a teacher and artist from Portland, Arkansas, when she asked:

How did you come to have Gerry as your channel? Is it possible to send out to the universe to have one's own connected spirit?

When Gerry first reached out to me, he had already learned a great deal about shamanism and conversing with spirit guides and power animals. But he had a strong desire to speak to an angel—specifically, his guardian angel. He'd been told that he had one of these when he was younger, and although we'd never spoken directly, it formed one of his strong core beliefs that he must have one.

Gerry pledged that he would find a way to communicate with me—if I would just tell him my name! He was not expecting the answer at that moment, but when he closed his eyes he very clearly saw the name *Margaret.* I had to spell it over several different times and in several different ways because it took him a while to believe that this was truly my name.

He felt moved to pick up a pad and write a letter to me, a method known as automatic writing. He wrote of all the troubles that were befalling his life at that time, and as he continued writing, he was surprised that he was starting to write a letter back to himself—his first channeled message from me. He was amazed that the message was showing him how he had been involved in the creation of all of his current life events; but there was no judgment or criticism in the message. The letter offered him insight into how other people in his life might be feeling about him and his actions. Throughout it all, he felt as though the message was carrying the energy of love.

Gerry asked me what I saw in him that made him so special— why did I choose him to communicate with? I said something that has become a running joke between us: there was nothing special about him at all! And, hopefully, when people saw that even he could do this, then they would finally realize that *anyone* could do it!

Yes, everyone already has a connected spirit and the ability to converse with their angels, but in order to use this ability it takes desire and openness. You'll want to try out different methods to see which one most appeals to you. Automatic writing is a technique that many people, including Gerry, have success with. Still others use oracle cards or angel cards or one of the many different communication aids that are out there. Just know that if you have the desire to communicate with us, then we share that desire as well, and we will do our best to bring the best tool to your attention!

Knowing that some people were still having problems, I asked Gerry to develop a special workshop on angel communication. He used his unique knowledge and skills to bring a new method into the world, resulting in the Angels & Shamans workshop. Through his classes, thousands of people have met their angels and now converse with them on a regular basis. (You can find the studio-recorded audio of this workshop on CD and digital download at www.gerrygavin.com.) During the workshop, Gerry draws upon his shamanic abilities and uses guided visualizations to create the perfect state for participants to be receptive to angelic messages. Once people become grounded with the earth, they cleanse and energize their chakras, release fear and grief from their heart, and finally are taken on a gentle journey to meet and converse with their angels.

∽

In order to be able to open up to deeper levels of spiritual communication, you need to let go of your fears and increase your trust. You might relate to *Sharon Duquette* from Tewksbury, Massachusetts, when she said:

I was so fearful when I first started hearing messages, and I am just finally accepting my gifts now. Why are we so hesitant to start believing? How can we reassure others that this is true and real without the fear of being judged?

This question really cuts to the core of why people find it difficult to open themselves up to spiritual communication. It does partially relate to the fear of being judged. But it goes deeper than how others will see you if you begin to talk about conversing with angels; it goes to your judgment of yourself. Many have trouble opening themselves up to angelic connection because they see themselves as being "unworthy" in some form or another. Even after they do get communication of some sort, they may dismiss it as being their imagination. So the first and most difficult step in opening up to any form of spiritual or "otherworldly" communication is trust in yourself! Know that you *are* getting this information and allow it to flow.

It is true, however, that some people are hesitant to personally communicate with angels because of regulations within their religious organizations. In some religions, it is not just considered taboo to attempt to communicate with angels or souls that have passed on, it may actually be considered a sin, blasphemy, or even proof of demonic possession! This is very sad. Please know that there are no restrictions regarding who is allowed to talk to angels and how that is allowed to take place. We are so interconnected with you and that is why you feel the pull toward us!

When you begin, it is best to spend some time communicating for yourself, asking the questions most important to helping you heal your life and setting yourself up for future happiness. Once you feel like the messages you are generating are accurate and true, it will give you the confidence to share these messages with others. Remember that like energy always attract like energy, so if you are worried that people will judge you, then you will probably attract people who will do so. If you think that there is a world of people eager to learn how to live a happy life, then you will attract those people to you instead. In the beginning of our work together, Gerry feared that he would attract doubters. Although he did attract some, he also saw that the overwhelming number of people who came to us for guidance left with lighter minds and joyful hearts. This caused him to feel joy in our work, and he then attracted more and more of those who sought a happier life of greater understanding.

Whether a person is an experienced communicator or just beginning to trust that they can talk to their angels, they often run into the issue brought up by *Louis Szabo,* an energy coach from Paris, France. He asked:

How can I tell the difference between what I would like to be the answer (my ego) and an actual angel's answer?

This is probably the most often asked question Gerry and I get when we are assisting people who are opening up to their intuitive, or psychic, abilities. The most important thing is to *feel* the message as you are getting it. If any of the words or the overall feeling of the message reflects an energy of judgment, blame, shame, or fear of any type, then that message is likely being filtered through your ego and is not coming directly from an angelic source.

For example, if you are fighting with your girlfriend and receive the message that you should dump her because she doesn't deserve someone who is as spiritually advanced as you are, then you have likely received that message from your ego. But if the message calls for calmness and opening yourself up to her perspective so that you can make decisions and hold a conversation from a place of loving compassion, then that would likely be your angelic message!

We will never judge, we will never blame, and we will never say that you or another are wrong or right. If you ask our advice and we suggest a certain course of action, we will never criticize you if you do not take that route. We will show love to you and we will show love to your enemy as well. We may speak of things having urgency, but we will never try to instill fear. We will always tell you to "fear not," and we will always urge you to love yourself—and to love others! The rule of thumb is that if the message is not coming from a place of unconditional love, compassion, and joy, then it is not coming from an angel.

∞

I am hopeful that you are now comfortable with the idea of contacting your angels for any help that you might need. It is also important to know that you can call upon angels to assist others; you don't have to wait for others to ask for the help themselves. As *Jill Lebeau,* a spiritual therapist and feng shui specialist from Berkeley, California, wrote:

> *On your radio show, I've heard you encourage us to ask for a "legion of angels" to assist us when we feel the need. I'd love to know what happens when we ask for a legion of angels to assist someone else. Sometimes I ask my angels to connect with someone else's angels, requesting that they deliver soothing, peaceful, nurturing, and loving energy to that person. What happens when I do this?*

Dear one, when you call upon angels to assist another, it is akin to praying for someone else. And prayer is exactly what you are doing here. You are not demanding, but requesting that a person be surrounded by angelic energy.

The word *legion* here might get somewhat misunderstood, thought of from the point of view of a human military. A legion would consist of thousands of soldiers, and a general would call upon however many were needed to ensure success and defeat the enemy. In the case of your prayer, the "enemy" is fear and other vibrations that are causing energetic drain.

When you call upon a legion of angels, you might receive the assistance of anywhere from a dozen to one hundred or more! The most important thing is not the number of angels but the vibration that those angels will create to protect an individual from energy drainage and to raise that person's vibration to a healing level. The number of angels needed depends on how many sources of energy are draining a person. Response to a prayer is virtually instantaneous, as angels will respond immediately and offer energy, regardless if they are involved in another task. As an angel finishes its work, it will be replaced by other angels so that the cycle of energetic protection and recharging will be completed.

Remember, however, that all of you are beings of free will. The person you are praying for can also continue to call in degenerative energy with the beliefs they are carrying. If a person is tied to fear, if their reality says that they are victims and not creators, then they are, in fact, creating that victim energy.

No matter what, however, we will continue to answer your requests for assistance whenever we are called upon!

∞

As a seeker, you strive to understand the essence of your energy and how it interrelates with that of angels and the Creator. While spiritual concerns are certainly important to you and to those who posed the questions in this book, there are also many people who will go through their entire lives without ever really wondering about these matters, and they are still contributing to the growth of the universe. So what causes this longing, *Marilyn Enness* wondered:

> *It seems that we spend a lot of personal resources and energy in working to know and connect with our angels. Why do we come to earth to learn about the spirit world? If we have all-knowing usage and understanding of our angels' services when we are in our spirit bodies, won't such matters be clearly evident when we cross back to spirit? Likewise, when we are in spirit, do we seek to learn about and understand the physical?*

It is true for so many that when you are on Earth, you spend a great deal of time trying to "remember" who you are in your spiritual state. When you are in your soul state, you understand all about your relationship to other souls, angels, and the Creator. It makes sense that, since you are going to return to that state, you could just wait till you get there to find out what is going to happen. So what then fuels the longing that so many humans have to understand what you perceive as the unknown?

I believe that I can sum it up in a single word: *connection*. When your soul places part of its energy into a physical body, you energetically still feel a connection to the whole of creation. That creates an energetic pull that makes you want to "stay in touch."

From the point of view of your human senses, think of when you live with someone you love. You know very well that you are going to be speaking with them when you see them that evening. However, in that situation, don't many of you still make it a point to speak with your loved ones at some time during the day? You desire to stay connected! On social media, which is so popular right now, you stay connected with all of the important people in your life, you share your thoughts and the things that you are doing, and sometimes you use it to receive or offer words of encouragement. You desire to know that others are well or see what they are doing. This urge stems from one of the things that your soul is always seeking to do, which is to live in the moment. When you speak during the day, it gives you the opportunity to then focus on the highlights of the day when you do see each other at night—or you can move on to entirely new topics and be totally present and in the moment for each other.

That is similar to your connection to your soul state from the physical state. You simply feel this sense of connection to something greater than what you are experiencing in your earthly existence. So you reach out for connection to that state; your consciousness seeks to understand your situation. When you come to the realization that you are part of something much greater—that you have a spiritual support team and are never alone, and that you have divinity within you and are definitely in the process of creating your earthly life—it gives you the ability to live in the moment as well. By reaching out to your higher self, spirit guides, and angels, you can access perspectives that allow you to live a much happier and less pressured life. So, most of the time, when you are reaching out to us, it is really not so much about understanding *us* as it is about getting a clearer sense of *yourself.*

Consider people in the process of searching out their genealogy. They do so because they are trying to have a sense of what kind of people preceded them, hoping that this will give them a little insight into themselves. In the same manner, many who are adopted or abandoned as a child want to know about their biological parents. It is natural to always be looking to better understand yourself. The more you understand, the happier you are able to be, so it is time well spent.

Know as well that your higher self is as interested in you as you are in it! When you are in your higher-self state, you are connected with all your incarnations, and you are focused on the experience and the adventure. Again, many of you see this in yourselves as humans as you seek to experience the thrill of skydiving, waterskiing, running with the bulls, or maybe swimming with the dolphins! Or in a different, more universal vein, becoming a parent, traveling to new places, and turning strangers into friends. You seek, as your soul seeks, to experience life to its fullest and to expand your experiences, knowledge, and emotions. That is why people love to lose themselves in a book or a movie as well—they are living that adventure at that moment.

So if you see your human existence in the same manner as your soul does, then you would see every moment of your life as one adventure leading you directly into another. You would be actively seeking out those adventures that bring you joy—for the attainment of joy is the ultimate desire of the soul.

❦

DESTINY, WILL, AND YOUR HIGHER SELF

> *"From the time you are born into your family of choice, you are essentially the star of your particular story, and everyone else is a supporting actor."*

There have been countless books written, songs penned, and movies filmed about what is the true nature of the human experience. Philosophers and theologians have debated whether your life is planned from start to finish or if it is just some cosmic joke in which nothing makes sense and no one knows what comes after. If your life is predetermined, then what is the purpose of living it? And if it isn't, then how do you know if you are making the "right" decisions as to how to live it? With so many questions plaguing mankind about this topic, it is not surprising to me that some of your questions centered on this as well, such as this one from *Andrea Mueller,* a spiritual teacher and retired nurse from Perth, Ontario. She asked:

Do we really have free will? Is there such a thing? Aren't we all guided by God? If we question people's decisions, aren't we questioning God's divine wisdom?

There is indeed free will, and it began with offering souls the determination of whether to live in light or to experience the polarity of the universe as a physical being. But free will is especially clear in your human state. While your higher self works alongside other souls to create different experiential possibilities for your incarnating consciousness, everything else that occurs from the moment of your birth is purely improvisation, both on your part and on the part of every other person in your life.

There is something very interesting that happens when you become a human being. As we are essentially talking about the "story" of your life, I find that it helps for understanding when I speak from the example of entertainment—your movies, in particular.

Your higher self creates the *backstory* of your human lifetime. As your higher self, you work with many souls, some of which are from your soul group (those souls created by your guardian angel in conjunction with the Creator) but others of which are not. You and these other souls design a rich and varied number of shared experiences for your incarnations that will allow all of you the greatest potential for growth. You jointly create a story of your roots— the legacy of emotions, talents, and wounds that have been passed down from generation to generation.

From the time you are born into your family of choice, you are essentially the *star* of your particular story, and everyone else is a *supporting actor.* Your only concern is what directly affects you. You want to be fed, you want to be nurtured, you want to be amused, and most of all you want to be loved! What is so interesting is that every other person in the world also regards themselves as the star of their story, and they see everyone else in their world as a supporting actor. Think of how complicated it would be to watch a movie in which every actor was the lead, and you had to keep track of every story and remember who's the lead and who are the supporting roles in each one as they moved back and forth!

This is similar to what is actually happening in your human world. But what makes it even more complicated is that there are billions of characters worldwide—and *no* script! Every day, every single character in your story, yourself included, wakes up with no idea of what the story will be that day. So you find yourself improvising through every day, looking for ways to jockey yourself into the position of feeling like the main lead.

This is free will at its greatest expression. You have the ability to respond to the situations in your life in a different way every day, and in so doing you are exercising your free will. When one speaks of God's plan for the world, know that the only plan the Creator has ever stated for you is that you would experience the magnificence of your divinity and your ability to be whatever you create!

~

In accepting that you have free will and that you are capable of affecting your life based on how you decide to express it, is it a given that you will be able to create the life that you desire? This was on the mind of *Tony Lauria,* a musician, vocalist, and performer from Grass Valley, California, who wrote:

> *Many teachers say that you can be, do, or have anything you desire. But after years of practicing the "allowing" techniques, attaining these things remains elusive for me. Is there some prearranged destiny that overrides your desires and keeps you on track with some higher order, no matter how resolved you are to move in the direction of your dreams? If not, what is the ultimate key to achieving one's reasonable goals?*

To answer the question of how to attain one's goals on earth, I must first explain how goals are set by your higher self.

As a soul, you are an immense energy! The interconnectedness of the huge energy of other souls and yours gives life to that which you call the universe. Your soul wishes to expand that energy by placing it in many different types of life forms, in many different points in the evolution that you call history.

To use a human financial analogy, your higher self invests its energy into different life forms much in the same manner as you would invest money in different types of stocks. You choose many different life forms in different geographic communities, socioeconomic situations, and periods of history because diversity of experience brings you greater opportunities; you have more options to expand and more ways to learn. You cannot be exactly sure how these soul investments will turn out, as so many variables affect their performance. But if your lifetimes make up a varied "portfolio," then you can be confident that in the long run, you'll expand your energy. With enough soul growth, your energy expands to a certain point where it "splits," and you are able to divide your soul into even more pieces that you can invest in even more new life forms; but you always remain the same higher self.

So your higher self takes big risks when it designs the energetic structure of certain lifetimes, hoping for a big return. And it plays it safe with the energetic structure of other lifetimes, minimizing risk and aiming for a slow and steady return. In other words, for the safest "return on your investment," you might put some of your soul energy into the incarnation of a child born into a loving and financially secure family. You know that there is a good chance for soul growth there, barring any unforeseen freewill choices. Then you might also invest some of your soul energy into a child born into poverty in a war-torn country, knowing that while there is heavy risk there is also great potential for even more incredible soul growth and profound lessons in love, compassion, and joy!

Sometimes a physical incarnation might have a desire for great energy expansion, yet is scared of the necessary risk involved. When you play it safe, you get predictable results, but won't attain the quantum leaps of soul growth that can happen when you take on the risks of the road less traveled. For example, let us say that your desire is to become a writer and a spiritual teacher, and you've been writing books in your spare time and engaging in practices of "allowing" the proper circumstances to be brought to you. However, the energy that manifests your desired goals will not come to you if you do not take the risk of bringing your teachings to the public's attention. If you are held back from moving out of your comfort zone by the fear of potential ridicule, then you won't take the risks that could bring a greater return. Indeed, many people do the same thing and stay in the same job for years, even when they're miserable, because they do not want to take their chances with the unknown.

At the time of planning a physical incarnation, your soul doesn't predetermine any of the exact details. There is no unchangeable outcome, or fate. Your goal is only to create a return of excess energy through all of your life forms, so you develop a plan with certain factors for growth and risk.

Souls planning incarnations with each other will look at factors like the family dynamic (stable or challenged), economic indicators (secure or shaky finances), and potential health factors (hereditary conditions or future challenges), as well as many other factors. Then soul groups will decide to team together to create opportunities for certain challenges that will allow for the greatest level of return in terms of soul growth and expansion.

Experiences of light bring security, stability, and appreciation of self-worth; in contrast, experiences of darkness bring insecurity, instability, and depreciation of self-worth. However, while both are creating experiences that generate growth, it is the riskiest investments that bring the most substantial return when they are turned around. So to increase the potential of your personal goals becoming your human realities, dear ones, it is often necessary for you to move out of your traditional comfort zones. You must expand the concept of merely *allowing* things to come to you and instead *actively invest* your energies into unique ideas to bring your dreams and subsequent goals into your reality.

⁓ ⚬ ⁓

Very often you will hear Gerry and me speaking about angels helping you to create the life of your dreams. After all, if you accept that your soul comes to Earth to discover different experiences and expand energy, then doesn't that mean that you are here in order to live out your dreams? In the physical world, every great creation starts as someone's dream, a person's emotional hope for the future.

But what role do angels play and what do you need to do as well to make this happen? *Katrin Navessi,* a singer/songwriter from Vienna, Austria, wrote to us to ask:

Why do human beings have dreams? Mine is to be a success-ful professional musician using my own songs and music. Is every dream that we have achievable or are some meant to stay dreams—and how can we be supported by our angels to make our dreams come true?

Dreams are the voice of your soul's desires coming through and trying to point you in the direction of the life that would make you the most joyful! There is a common refrain from many human beings that they are working a job just to pay the bills while their true passion is in something different. When you have a passion for something that you are not doing, it becomes a dream as you devote time and energy toward it, imagining the joy it would bring.

A passionate dream has the greatest potential of becoming a reality when you have already put your own creative force to work in trying to manifest it. If your focus is steady, your intention is clear, and you are taking action toward making your dream a reality, then you can raise your vibration to a higher level and attract more opportunities to you by asking for a legion of angels to assist you in this endeavor. Do note that part of making your dream a reality is *taking action* toward your dream. While asking angels for assistance and focusing your thoughts may lead you to the circumstances and people that may help you, you may find yourself unprepared to seize the opportunity if you haven't taken action in preparation for your dreams becoming reality. For example, if you ask for help from your angels to be a successful musician, we may be able to create the framework to bring you into a situation where you meet an influen-tial person in the record industry. Yet it would be hard for us to go further in creating that reality if you haven't also been putting in the effort to practice your instrument or write songs.

When Gerry wrote *Messages from Margaret,* he did not know that he was going to become a Hay House author. I asked him to share my message with the world, so he channeled my thought form into words, and then chose the avenue of self-publishing a book. In order to make the words available to anyone who desired to read them, he found a company that would produce a book in both print and electronic forms on demand. While he was still not sure how to get my message to the world at large, he continued taking action toward that goal by bringing the book to a local mind-body-spirit expo, as that seemed like an appropriate venue to give him the experience of sharing the book with others.

What Gerry did not know was that we angels were working behind the scenes to create a framework for potential opportunities for the book to grow. He trusted my opinion as to the booth he should rent, although it didn't seem like the best location on paper. As a result, he met a wonderful woman, Valerie Paik, who was assisting at a booth across the way. She was drawn to the cover of the book, purchased it, and stayed up all night reading it. Valerie loved the book so much that she brought Gerry to the attention of her mentors, Ariel and Shya Kane, whom she was assisting at the expo. They asked Gerry to be a guest on their Internet radio show *Being Here,* and that episode was heard by Alexandra Gruebler, who sells the international rights for Hay House. She in turn brought the book to the attention of Hay House CEO, Reid Tracy, who asked Gerry to allow Hay House to republish it. By taking simple actions toward his dream, and trusting I was there assisting in the process, Gerry turned words on a computer screen into a book accessible to a worldwide audience, translated into seven different languages.

Whatever the process by which your dream comes to fruition, it is very important that you stay steadfast and assist us by taking action that will help us to manifest your energies into the world. Don't focus on worries that create a repelling energy! Remember the power of Afformations and think to yourself, *Why is it so easy for my music to come to the attention of the world?* Whatever your dream, you can create an Afformation to fit that which you desire to achieve! It is also important to see your work as a service for mankind, regardless of the scope of your dream or the outcome; that will draw success to you, since it is coming from an energy of love!

There is something else that is moving people toward trying to align their soul to their dreams. They seek a greater connection to something that they can sense, something they know is greater than just this human experience. **John Holland,** a world-renowned psychic medium, sought-after speaker, spiritual teacher, and best-selling author of *Born Knowing* and *Psychic Navigator,* referred to this energetic occurrence when he astutely asked:

> *In the past, many people have come to see me, whether private-ly or in a public platform, in the hopes that I could connect with a loved one that has crossed over into the Spirit World. Now I am noticing more and more people are asking also about their own spirituality and how they can connect more deeply to God, Source, Spirit, or their own intuitive abilities, which are beginning to open suddenly within them. Why is this happening more now? Is there some sort of cosmic or universal shift that is happening on the planet? What advice would you give to these people who are desperately seeking answers?*

Through years of evolution and soul growth, mankind *is* shift-ing. One of the biggest aspects to that shift is that more and more people are moving into more of a do-it-yourself world. As mankind becomes less trusting of the establishments that they have created, they are finding that they would prefer to learn how to do things on their own. They seek to do this because it is more rewarding, both in personal satisfaction and financially. But the underlying reason that people are moving to this DIY mentality is that it is empowering!

This, John, is why you are seeing these questions coming up more and more within your work, because you have always been about empowering people rather than empowering yourself. For years, you have taught people that they are all born psychic! You have taught them that they are spirits who are having a physical experience, and you teach others how to develop their own psy-chic abilities. They trust you and know that it is your desire to help them to grow!

At this point in the evolutionary cycle, people are seeking to take back their power. Even though they are not fully aware of why, mankind is seeking to tap into some of the knowledge that they have already acquired at the soul level in order to make their lives easier. On a human level, they are seeking to get a better handle on what things in their life they should invest their energy in. Just as human beings look to ways to streamline or simplify their lives so that they can achieve optimal performance and growth, this is totally consistent with the desire of the higher self and other souls to expand the universe in the quickest and easiest ways possible. It is also consistent with one other aspect of soul growth and expansion—and that is to, above all, seek to experience joy!

There are many things that you are able to learn when you tap into your soul state and your higher self. World-renowned intuitive counselor, psychic medium, and best-selling author of *The Map: Finding the Magic and Meaning in the Story of Your Life,* **Colette Baron-Reid,** offered a wonderful question that takes a sneak peek at just a few of them:

What are some of the untapped abilities that human beings have yet to discover about themselves? Are there any methods you suggest for us to enhance abilities such as greater access to creativity, aligning our intention with manifestation with more ease, or the power to stretch time and pull information from the future?

One of the great challenges for many human beings is tapping into their abilities, as they often feel blocked by self-doubt, fear, anger, and regret. So when we come to look at the topic of the "untapped" abilities of the human race—and how that relates to reaching out to the higher self—it makes for an exciting question for me to respond to indeed!

So let's begin by starting with a very basic supposition: You are all energetic beings that are made up of complex cellular structures. Giving life or breath to that structure is *consciousness.* This is the essence of what you truly are and this is often referred to as the soul.

This consciousness is the true underlying power source of all things. Think for a moment about all the electrical devices in your house. Your TV looks different from your toaster and your heater has a different function from your washing machine, but they all work by using the same electrical force that you have harnessed so it can be shared with all of these vessels. The force that allows you to walk around without a power cord is the same force that inhabits the electric lines that power all these other items as well: namely, electromagnetic charges! Now you can break that word down into *electro*, which means having an energetic current, and *magnetic*, which means a positive or negative charge that will attract like energy to it!

But let's just back up a moment and realize that the electricity that powers your toaster comes from a current in your house, which comes from a wire connecting it to a substation that powers your neighborhood, which is in turn powered by a much larger electrical generation center, which channels back to some major source of electricity production that is connected to the natural order: the sun, the wind, the movement of water through a dam, or the burning of some type of fuel. Energy all originates from some natural life force, and that is the same energy that is in you and all around you.

This energy is constant and does not understand the human concepts of time and space. It cannot be destroyed; all it will do is morph into some other form. So if all things emanate from the same energetic source, then how can you stretch or collapse time at will and create the future that is in alignment with that which you desire? The answers to this are so much easier than you might imagine, and I say this because you are already using many of these techniques but you just have not been paying them any mind.

Your perception of the energy you are expending determines your perspective on time. When you are enjoying what you are doing and your vibration is high, then time seems to move more quickly. You may think that a clock moves at a steady rate and that time seeming to move quickly is just an illusion, but it is time *itself* that is the illusion. In that same vein, think about when you have to do something that you don't enjoy. Can you remember days where the clock just did not seem to move? Consider the adage that a watched pot never boils; it is because you are looking at the pot with anticipation and desire, and the time can't come fast enough! But again, have there not been times that you have accidentally let things burn on the stove because you became involved in something else and time just flew?

Most of you would agree with the phrase "time flies when you are having fun" and perhaps another that says "joy is fleeting!" By that I mean that when you are in a joyful state, your vibration is so high within those milliseconds, seconds, minutes, and hours that you are not even aware that they are passing. You are involved in the *energy* of the experience and not in time. So that, dear ones, becomes the secret for how you can harness time for your overall benefit and well-being.

It starts with a thought. It starts with a thought about something that makes you happy—something that brings you joy! You think that thought and smile, and then you hold the energy of the feeling until such time that you begin to feel the smile growing by itself and the joyful thought morphing into another joyful thought. Then you allow that new joyful thought to enter your mind and you intentionally smile along with that thought, until that thought begins to smile along with you. And by the third or fourth joyful thought that has come to your mind, you will find your emotional state shifting to a place of joy—and as it does time will begin to shift with it. That which vibrates faster moves time more quickly with it. Now that is not to say that a joyful person can force the sun to rise or set any faster. However, the joy that they will feel between that sunrise and sunset will be so sublime that it will feel like time has gone by in a blink of an eye.

Is it not that way with your children? I so often hear humans say that you have only blinked your eyes and your children have gone from little babies to married with children of their own. Yet I am sure that "joy is fleeting" is not what comes to mind when your baby is up all night crying or your teen tells you that they just wrecked your car! When you are in the vibration of that moment, time seems endless. But at their first school recital, birthday parties, high school graduation—and most certainly at their wedding or when they are moving away—you will find that their entire lifetime seems to be passing before your eyes, and you realize how time has and is flying by!

So whenever you are involved in a task that has you feeling like you just can't stand its drudgery, think of all those current joyful thoughts in your life. I would even suggest that you begin to keep a journal of sublime memories that you can call upon when time seems to be pressing down on you!

As for pulling from the future and aligning your intention with manifestation, this works in a similar manner. Like energy attracts like energy. In order to pull something that you would like from the future—which is to say the potential of your creative manifestation—you need to make sure that you are making clear notes of where that energy is currently present in your life. In other words, you need to be aware of those things in your present life that bring you joy; then take it one step further and make it your intention, each and every day, to set your dominant desires to being open to discovering joy in every single moment and every single experience of the day. Celebrate the joys of others as well, because when you are celebrating someone else's joy, then you are coming from a clear place of knowing that there is more than enough to go around.

When you focus on creating joy, this will automatically enhance your creative energy because when your overall desire is to create joy, then your energy is fueled by joy, which then, in turn, jump-starts your creative process!

≈

One of the primary purposes of your incarnations is to give the soul the opportunity to experience joy regardless of the situations in which you might find yourself. This is not always the easiest to do, but happily there are people devoting their lives to helping others in this task. One of these people is happiness coach and spiritual speaker **Jennifer Kass**, who shared some interesting information about her soul mission:

I had a clarifying experience when I spoke to Doreen Virtue on her radio show in 2012 and again at a conference in 2013. She channeled the angels' messages to me and said that I have a global-political-spiritual mission. Her advice was that, as an Indigo soul, I must learn how to change the way I relate to the world before trying to change the world. From your perspective, what do you feel is the most important thing we do or experience in this lifetime while we are in a physical body?

In helping people to achieve greater states of happiness, and in so doing raise their vibration as well as that of the planet, you are helping to respond to your personal global-political-spiritual mission, dear one, and asking this question helps me to expand how others can do so as well. As human beings, you tend not to identify with the world, but rather you identify with very small sections with which you interact. If I were to ask most people who they were, I would most likely get an answer like: "I am a woman" (or another gender); "I am a daughter, mother, and sister" (or some other familial connections); "I am a New Yorker" (or other location); and "I am Jewish" (or another religion). You might further identify yourself by your social class or by the work that you perform (stockbroker, plumber, etc.). Very likely, the descriptors would be in the order that the person saw as most important. Yet very few people will identify themselves as "residents of the earth." People will feel an attachment to their family, their neighborhood, their city, their country. They will feel an affiliation with their school, their fraternal organization, even their favorite sports team. But for most there is no connection to the planet that was created to offer you all of the things necessary for your physical form to survive.

The planet gives you food, water, sunlight, and the air that you breathe. It even provides all of the natural resources that you now use to produce your electrical systems with which you power the amazing technology you have created. But most do not see these things as being generously provided by your host planet. You instead identify it with the companies that have harvested the food or the fuels or even the water. This disconnect is one of the things that causes you to have conflict with protecting the earth as well as disconnection with people from other parts of the world. When you see the earth not as the provider of all that you need to live, but rather as a globe with imaginary lines that separate where you are from where others are, then you do not see *them* as being the same as *you* or recognize that all of you are reliant on this same planet.

One of the most important things that everyone can learn, as part of your time here in this physical world, is that it is all interconnected. Without making light of any individuals' voices or the work they do on this planet, in truth *everyone* is involved in a global-political mission and needs to learn to change the way that they are relating to the world. The word *world* pertains not to the world that one individually knows, but rather to everyone who lives on this planet. They are all souls who have come here to share this experience and help each other to grow. This means that every person from every race and every country and every economic status needs to be regarded with the same love and compassion as those whom you already love! It means that as you pray or meditate, it would do you good to pray for every being on the planet and not just those that you know—even those that you might perceive as your enemy! It means that when you recycle, or do things to preserve the environment, you are not only preserving your country but the whole planet as well.

Your physical environment is not only your body, it is everything around you that supports that body to eat, to breathe, and to experience beauty and peace. Being in tune with your own soul and the soul of the planet is one of the most important things you can do. Learn to love the world, and it will help you to love yourself in ways you never imagined!

❧

THE PATH
OF LEAST
RESISTANCE

> *"One of the most common misunderstandings is thinking that the life that you are currently leading is not already a part of your path and purpose."*

"What is my path and purpose?" In our more than two decades of doing readings, Gerry and I receive this question more frequently than any other. The exact answer varies for every person, of course, touching upon the personal desires and goals of each soul who comes into a particular incarnation. But as I have said in previous chapters, your circumstances and the direction of your plan may change based on your freewill actions and the influence of family, friends, and romantic relationships. It is easy to say that wherever you are in life is exactly where you are supposed to be, so spend every day in joyous expression of the person that you are—and that would be a correct answer!

But those who ask this question are not necessarily satisfied with this statement. What they really want to know is the answer to what the soul is asking: How can the experience of this human body help my soul to grow in the greatest way possible and help other souls to grow in the greatest way possible? While the answer that I have already given to you will work in expanding the energy of the soul, I would like to offer a few suggestions as to how to harness the power of the experiences you've already encountered and identify ways you can expand your soul's energy and your current earthly joy at the same time. In so doing we will also identify potential ways that you might be able to create work that will support your passions and interests.

One of the most common misunderstandings is thinking that the life that you are currently leading is not already a part of your path and purpose. Everything that you have been doing from the moment of your birth to this moment, as you are reading this book, has been part of your soul's design to draw to you experiences to help you along your path. The parents you were born to, the community where you live, your family's chosen religion, and your economic situation at birth were all chosen by you as you created the template for your soul's plan of growth.

In 2013 Gerry and I created a Soul-Based Business course in order to assist individuals in figuring out the type of work that would bring them joy along with supporting a joyous lifestyle. As part of that program, one of the exercises the participants do is to list the strengths and skills they've developed over their lifetime; in doing so, we identify the trajectory that their soul has already established. We ask the participants to look at their lives in five-year increments and think upon the people and situations that offered them the most love and support as well as those that offered them the greatest challenges. Then they write down what they learned and what skills they developed from each set of circumstances. Finally, they give thanks to the people involved in both the light and dark periods, often coming to the realization that they've learned even more from their challengers than their supporters.

When you begin to look at your own life from this perspective, you can begin to see a pattern emerging. It is always a pattern of growth, even though you might not see it that way at the time. You learn from every experience you have, including those you judge to be mistakes; in fact, you learn *more* from them.

In speaking about mistakes, my favorite analogy comes from your movies and TV shows. You'll hear the director calling out for "take one" at the beginning of an individual scene that is taking place, often with the number climbing higher as they film a shot over and over. What the director is looking for is the best possible "take," or version of that scene, to tell a story. The takes that aren't quite right, that do not tell the story in the manner that the director had hoped, are not used in the final cut of the scene. You might call these "mis-*takes*."

This is how it is in your life. Imagine that your higher self is the producer of the story of this incarnation, and he hired your consciousness (which is the soul energy that empowers your body) to direct your playing of this character. Your higher self and your consciousness are constantly working alongside the improvised script of your life to help you in your interpretation of this role called you! In doing the exercise of remembering your supporters and detractors and what you learned from them, you would be like an actor who studies his backstory to understand what made him who he is today and what his motivation is. If your motivation is experiencing as much joy as possible, then you bring that into how you play yourself, and it will become a part of your character. And I use the word *character* to mean not just the person you are playing but also to mean the very core of the behaviors and beliefs that are "you." Sometimes the word gets used to describe the positive behaviors that you find very desirable, which is often someone who is joyful and filled with life!

In fact, a "character filled with immense character" is just the way that I would describe **Pam Grout**, the author of the #1 *New York Times* bestseller *E-Squared: Nine Do It-Yourself Energy Experiments That Prove Your Thoughts Create Your Reality*. She describes herself as someone who believes the world is a beautiful place, people are noble, and anything is possible. Her path led her to explore every one of the world's continents as a travel writer before being called to write a book that would help down-to-earth people see that you can create your own reality and have fun while living your purpose. Her questions are delightfully Pam:

One of my four main goals is unceasing joy—am I as crazy as people sometimes think I am? How can all of us lighten up here on planet Earth? How can we have more fun?

If *crazy* means being incredibly funny, seeing the fun in everything, and expecting that every new day is going to be the best day ever—then yes, you are crazy! And I don't think that it would be an error to say that most people would love some of that "crazy" in their lives! When you constructed your path, you wanted to create a career that would allow you to do the things you loved. If you were to look at your soul's trajectory, you would recognize that three major things brought you joy: travel, writing, and sharing stories to allow others to feel your joy! Your challengers helped you to develop your dreams, your helpers aided you in developing your writing skills and sense of humor, and this path culminated in your wonderful career.

There are some definite things that you can do to "lighten up," as you put it, and I would love to share some of them with everyone here.

— **Find joy!** Even if you feel that you have nothing to smile about, physically smile—and keep doing it until your brain thinks that there must be a reason that you are doing so. It will kick in the chemicals to make it happen naturally. Then laugh, even if nothing is humorous. Eventually your brain will conclude that you must be enormously happy, and again it will produce the brain chemicals to justify your laughing, and it will start laughing with you!

— **Look up!** Lean your head back and look up. If you haven't done it for a while, you are going to hear some cracking in your neck—and that is a good thing. It means that some hard tissue is breaking up and some flexibility is coming back. Looking up affects your brain chemistry as well. There is a reason why people say that "things are looking up" or someone "looked really down." How you hold your head will determine how your brain thinks that you are feeling—not to mention that you are allowing us to see your beautiful face.

— **Open your arms to receive!** Again, I know that you may think this is simplistic, but when you are worried or harried, you tend to bring your arms in closer to your body. Subconsciously, your brain is protecting your heart center. If you throw open your arms while you are looking up, it is a clear signal that you are ready to receive, and you will feel the energy come into you—I promise this! Don't do it for just a second; allow your arms to stay open until you feel the shift in energy. You may notice that a slight smile might come to you, or that you begin to sense energy coming into your chest region.

∽

Sometimes, even when you are doing things to lighten up your energy and learn more about what your path and purpose might be, something happens that energetically "pulls the rug out" from under you. Such was the case for *Stella Hu,* an enterprise risk manager from Toronto, Ontario. She found that transition sometimes comes from within you—but sometimes also outside of you. Stella writes:

> *My position was recently impacted by company reorganization and I ended a significant relationship, all at the same time. Some-how, I feel I'm ready to move on into something new. What is the deeper meaning of this loss to me? Is the universe reminding me to realign my life? How do I get angelic guidance from now on? What am I born into this world to manifest?*

When life hits you out of the blue, it can be hard to recognize that you are actually the one who has orchestrated these changes to allow you to grow or to free you from situations that are not bring-ing you joy. Very often people will feel a stirring in them that tells them that they are ready for a change. This stirring is the voice of your soul, trying to lead you into the direction of that which would create a more joyful experience for you—while allowing you to take your unique voice and ideas into the world for the greater good.

This is what you felt, Stella, and what so many others who are reading this book feel as well. But fear often gets in the way of doing the things that you know in your heart are in your best interest. So that sets up a push/pull of energy around you, and you find yourself in a state of inertia. But when your desire to connect with your soul and its direction is strong and you ask for angelic aid, you find the courage and support to close the energies that are no longer serving you so you can be free to move into new directions.

Gerry found himself facing a similar situation in his life. For years, our work was a side job for him. He worked from the bottom up in the newspaper business, from delivering papers to people's homes in the middle of the night, reporting on town council meetings and basketball games, writing obituaries, selling advertising that helped local businesses and the newspaper to grow, and eventually becoming the publisher of the largest community newspaper company in the media capital of the world, New York City. During this time, he had this other life in which he was channeling my messages and providing shamanic services to people throughout the world.

At the time, Gerry did not realize that all of the skills he was developing through his newspaper career were also bringing him the knowledge and confidence to do this work with me. He learned to ask questions as a newspaper reporter. Sales taught him how to communicate with people and see how helping a business to grow could be a win-win situation rather than just self-serving competition. As he covered high school sports and wrote obituaries, he saw the energy of youth in its "glory days" and compared that to what people actually find important when they pass; often this led him to ponder how he wished to be remembered. Publishing brought out his voice into the world, and he was able to bring topics like alternative healing, caregiving, and environmental issues to the attention of the mainstream audience of his papers.

Even though Gerry was in awe of the amazing synchronicities that occurred with the publishing of his first book, he was still frightened to make a move from working in publishing full-time to working on spreading our message full-time. He wanted so much for that to happen, so he asked for our help—and we responded. One day he found that his job had been eliminated, just as Stella writes about hers. When it happened, he'd not only desperately needed the time to write this book but also needed to see that he would be just as secure working in this world as in the other.

So very often, when changes come into your life that set it in a new trajectory, it is because you have asked angels for help in moving you into the direction of your greatest joy. When you are standing in the way of yourself, your soul desires gently "shove" you onto the path that you have been asking for all along. Just keep talking to your angels and asking for guidance when this happens and know that you are always supported if you are asking for help. Please don't forget to ask for the legion of angels for help in raising your vibration. In this way, you will better hear the frequency of your higher self when it shares with you a potential "higher calling."

～

Years before Gerry first spoke with me, he was told by a psychic/psychologist friend that he was going to enter a partnership with someone that would not end, and it would be the most amazing experience of his life. Although Gerry never guessed that this was going to be a partnership with an angel, he felt there was something he knew he had to do, something that could potentially change the world. Whenever he would have these thoughts, it would either frighten him or cause him to shy away from his "ego trip." *Cherie Ninomlya*, a life coach from Chiba, Japan, knows this feeling all too well! She writes:

How can I deal with the fear that I have something urgent to do in this life, and I will not be able to identify it before I pass on? How do we raise our vibrations so we can hear our angels and guides?

My first advice to you, dear Cherie, is to stop fearing that which you feel is your calling. Fear is a paralyzing emotion. I would like to demonstrate this with a story that recently happened to Gerry.

Gerry was at a store with his girlfriend, Gail, when she was about to make a significant purchase. She was trying to make the right decision by weighing the features and benefits of each of the many options she liked. The very logical but pushy salesman kept telling her that there were only three factors she needed to consider: appearance, price, and comfort with the item. But Gail doesn't make decisions that way; instead, she uses all of her senses, touching it, and sometimes even smelling it. She is much like the horses that she so loves because they also take in information from all of their senses, sometimes "breathing in" signals from things around them.

The salesman then said, in a rather condescending manner, that she must be a perfectionist and began to tell her of the "three P's," as he called it. He said that *perfectionism* leads to *procrastination,* because you don't make a decision out of fear of making the wrong one, which then leads to *paralysis,* or making no decision at all. But the one P that he had forgotten about is outside *pressure,* of which he was certainly providing a significant amount. It causes people to have difficulty in listening to their inside voice, and Gail's internal messengers felt pressured to process the information she was taking in at the speed the salesman desired her to take it all in. The sensory information being processed by her enteric (gut) nervous system and central (brain) nervous system became blocked by the conflict between "logical" and "gut" thinking, and she quickly developed a migraine.

Gail was totally justified in taking the time to process things in the manner she desired, while the salesman was trying to create an unreal sense of urgency to close the sale and ease his own impatience. However, the situation does lend itself to helping understand what you are going through when you are feeling that there is something urgent that you must do (a sensation of impatience that you are creating). Your logic may be in conflict with your gut, and your fears may be overriding your trust in your soul. There is this voice inside of you—perhaps your angel, perhaps your higher self—that is asking you to allow yourself to open up your senses to hear what it is saying. You try to do so, but you may not completely trust your senses when you get messages because you don't want to be mistaken. You keep waiting until the message is undeniable. In the meantime there are all kinds of pressures from the world around you: Never mind about that pipe dream; there are real things you have to take care of here! That conflict causes a feeling of "energetic paralysis" inside of you, and that turns what started as a gentle reminder from your angels into a feeling of imagined urgency inside of you.

The energy of urgency only occurs in you because you are translating your personal purpose, or thing you are trying to accomplish, into physical time. Your soul knows there are no time boundaries and no way to get anything wrong; everything is happening in the right and proper time. When you are feeling urgency, it helps to open up to your angels and to say the Afformation, "Why is it so easy for me to know deep inside that everything is unfolding for me at exactly the right time!" If you are still having trouble, I would suggest that you look into Gerry's Angels & Shamans workshop to help you get as grounded as possible and learn how to open up to your angels' communication.

Gerry's feelings of urgency around writing this book are further proof that everything happens at the right time. I kept trying to reassure him that all would be well, but he was concerned that the flow of information from me was slow and sometimes even strained. Then he realized that he wouldn't have been able to include recent experiences in this book, like Gail's visit to the store, if he had completed it sooner.

When you can feel that you are straining with the flow, it doesn't always mean that the flow is being hampered. Sometimes it is just coming to you from a different direction. Sometimes it is coming from the Path of Least Resistance!

∽

What if you see something in someone else that they don't see; or, even if they see it, they aren't doing anything to bring it to the forefront? Can you help others find their path and purpose? This is a common dilemma encountered by many people in the healing arts as well as parents, coaches, doctors, personal trainers, and teachers of any kind. I will let *Tina Sanchoo,* an international certified success and lifestyle coach in New York City, New York, explain in her own words:

As a success coach, I work to help people reach their highest potential, and I often find that I am more excited by a person's potential than they are. Over time I am able to change that, but is there a way to help my clients to jump-start that energy more quickly?

I am sure that so many people who are reading this book can relate to this concern. Perhaps you feel that your son or daughter is squandering their abilities. Or maybe you might be a supervisor at a workplace and can see so much more potential in workers than they can. Or it could even be that you are in a relationship and keep trying to convince your loved one that they should reach out to use talents they don't even acknowledge!

The problem is that others do not see themselves through your eyes. They can view themselves only through the prism of their own experiences. They have written their narratives in a very different way than you have because you see the potential in them that they cannot see. Perhaps a person has encountered a lifetime of being told that they are not talented or been advised to limit their talents to things that guarantee success or security. It is easy in such cases to understand why they are less likely to recognize the unique gifts they have to offer to the world.

Remember also that like energy attracts, so you will often attract clients that have similar skills, or issues, as you; or they may have some characteristic that you most wished you possessed. When someone comes to you with the talents you wish you had, you automatically see the potential in them because you already know what you could do with those gifts!

Many teachers will use the example of Abraham Lincoln to show that anyone can come from humble means and still become successful—for a more recent success model, they might speak of Oprah Winfrey or Steve Jobs. But the fastest way to get someone excited about their potential path is to offer them success stories about people who came from a similar background or their current situation. It doesn't even have to be someone that you have personally worked with; you can do a little online research to locate appropriate anecdotes. When people know that there are others out there who are very similar to them who have been successful, it assists in actually converting their belief system about their potential.

When you find common ground with someone who started out just like you and is now successful, you can jump-start your sense of potential because you can *see* that it can be done—finding and living one's path and purpose is not just an elusive dream!

VIBRATION AND THE PROCESS OF MANIFESTATION

> *"The first part of being able to consciously manifest is to realize that you are already manifesting."*

Once someone has accepted that they have already manifested the energy that created the life they are currently living, the next question we often get is, "How can I change what I am manifesting so that I can create a life that reflects what I want?"

The first part of being able to consciously manifest is to realize that you are already manifesting. You are presently on a path that is allowing you to gain the skills and understanding you need to bring your unique energy to the world—and the work that you are already doing is a part of it. From the time that you are born, you are actively involved in working alongside others to create the story of your life, but until you become consciously aware that you are the author, then you will continue to believe that God or some other "ghostwriter" is controlling your story and you are just playing along.

One person who helps others to rewrite the story of their lives is *Tiffany Nightingale,* a narrative therapy counselor from Hamilton, New Zealand. She writes:

> *I have become increasingly aware of the power that rests within the way we story our lives. There is healing power in developing an awareness of these stories and taking hold of the narratives we tell in order to truly become the author of our own lives. This awareness is opening into a rich source of transformation for myself and the people I assist. What kind of knowing is it that is arising within me? How can it increase my capacity to help and to heal?*

Everything that human beings do is based around the stories you create in your lives. Each day you arrive at work, you tell stories about home, and when you get home you tell stories about work. You listen to songs, which are stories set to music. You watch films and television shows that tell stories of others' experiences, whether real or fictional, and you even devote hundreds of channels to telling only certain types of stories. The story of your past as a civilization is told in legends and history, while scientists and psychics alike tell stories about what will be happening in the future.

You are also constructing stories about yourself. Maybe you tell yourself the story about how you aren't successful because you didn't have rich parents to help you the way others did, or the story of how messed up the dating scene is, filled with shallow people who won't even give someone like you a chance. Perhaps you have a story about how kids, music, food, and everything else were so much better when you were young. Along with all this, you might tell yourself stories in which you are not good enough, rich enough, smart enough, or skilled enough to be what you might like to be. Most of mankind fills their lives with these types of stories.

Your life as a human is rich with stories at every moment of your day because that is the way in which information is collected and disseminated. So it is important to take note of the types of stories that you are telling and focus on the right ones. What are you saying and thinking about yourself and about others? Are they sad stories? Complaining stories? Are they designed to make another person fearful or anxious? Do they say damaging things about others? Or are you telling funny stories, uplifting stories, informative stories, helpful stories, loving stories? As you begin to notice what types of stories you are telling, you will have a better sense of what overall energy you are attracted to—and are attracting *to* you!

If you want to change the energy that you are attracting, then you begin by changing the story. However, the quality and skill of the storyteller influences the power behind the tale. Imagine the same story being told by two different people: One person speaks in a bland, boring way. Although the facts get conveyed, it is nothing you would ask to hear again. Then another person recounts the story in a voice filled with passion and color, weaving details together in an experience that is emotional and personal. Perhaps there is added humor that allows you to experience the essence of joy, so that even a problematic experience becomes engaging. When that person speaks, you tune in so you don't miss a word, and you look forward to their next story.

Since the stories you tell define the life you see yourself as having, the key to becoming a master manifester is to become a masterful storyteller. Remember that everything is created from some form of cellular structure, so if you share positive, uplifting, and informative stories, then you are moving toward manifesting cells that will take you in the direction of positive, uplifting, and informative experiences. When you craft stories, the details hit the energy field where we angels assist in making matter from thought. Then one set of the thought cells that make up your story will attract other cells that desire to tell the same kind of story. Then other cells will bond with them until such time as your story has created a more dense cellular structure, and it becomes a thought *form*—matter that is created from thought.

The following practice is wonderful to do with a trusted person who shares your beliefs: Take turns telling each other about how wonderful an experience it is to have the things you would like to manifest into your life. Describe all the rich details as though what you want to take place has already happened. You might want to make a recording of yourself so you can review your message; see if you get yourself excited as you listen. The universe responds the same as you do to an interesting story, so the more enthusiastic you are when you are crafting and telling your story, the greater your power of manifestation!

∞

What if you've been trying to create a lifestyle of love and appreciation for yourself and others, but no matter how positive you are or what you do, you cannot seem to energetically move forward toward that manifestation? *Amanda Bingham,* a traffic coordinator in specialty TV in Uxbridge, Ontario, writes:

> *After a certain point, is it possible that your vibration will not recover? Say you've had numerous unfortunate events happen to you over the years, could you reach a certain age (I am 49) and always continue to attract major key disasters? Or, worse, never attract what you truly want? What if this happens even if you are very aware of your thoughts and you change them to be only positive thoughts; will negative vibrations continue to rub up against you? If so, what can I do about it to get rid of this vibration so that I can attain success?*

Many people feel stuck when they draw the same negative patterns into their lives. They're doing all the "right" things, trying as hard as they can to cultivate a positive mind-set, and they're still unable to move forward. This happens because of a situation known as *soul loss.* When you lose part of your personal energy, you are unable to function at your highest potential and you draw energy to yourself that is similar to the energy that caused the soul loss in the first place! Almost everyone has encountered some level of soul loss.

While this might sound like something a logical mind would have difficulty believing, please allow me to explain it from a place of down-to-earth sensibility. Let us begin with the very basic truth that there is an energy that inhabits you and keeps you alive. This life-force energy, also known as your soul or your consciousness, is a small portion of the major energy that is your higher self.

Everything you experience is processed through the body, absorbed into the consciousness, then uploaded to the higher self. However, in a very traumatic situation, sometimes the energy of the experience moves so quickly that it flies through your aura (the energetic space around your body) and into the time and space around it. In other cases, your brain will anticipate a trauma and intentionally send conscious energy to a "safe place," where it can be recovered later. In either case, soul loss occurs during a time when a person feels a sense of being totally powerless within a certain situation, and this causes an extreme loss of energetic power through the solar plexus. Some people have described the feeling as similar to being punched in the stomach.

Soul loss creates an energetic void in your life-force energy. It is a fact of physics that energy will always seek to fill a void and that like energy attracts. Because soul loss imprints a void with the energy of the trauma that caused it, you then continue to attract the like energy of that trauma. This is why people experience patterns of behavior, even though they may be doing everything to break the cycle. It is not about a fault in their actions or thoughts; it is about the energy that is being attracted to the void.

As a void attracts the energy of similar experiences, this will often cause repeated occasions of soul loss. As this occurs, your soul energy, your life force, becomes depleted. To understand this, think for a moment about the battery of your cell phone. When it is fully charged you are able to use it to its full capacity. You can download a film or music, while taking photos and talking on the phone and more! But as your energetic charge begins to wane, you become more and more limited in the things that you are able to do. Finally, your phone will alert you to when your battery reaches too low of a limit and will prevent you from doing anything else to preserve the remaining charge.

Your brain acts in this same manner when it comes to monitoring your life-force energy. It takes quite a bit of energy just to operate your body; there are so many systems that need support. So when you are drained of soul energy, your physical energy will be depleted as well. Your brain will try to limit you from activities that may put you in a position where you are not in full control of your energy, or where you could potentially be powerless. Many people who encounter a substantial depletion of soul energy will experience adrenal failure, as the body is constantly under stress. Others will develop panic disorders as the brain tries to keep the person from doing anything where it cannot be in complete control. Substantial soul loss can also lead to addiction, just as addiction can be the cause of further soul loss as well! All people who are going through post-traumatic stress disorder are feeling the effects of soul loss!

The wonderful thing is that just as soul pieces can be lost, they can also be recovered. What may have been lost in a lifetime of trauma can be reclaimed by you within just a few hours. The same shamanic practices that allowed the original people of this planet to recover them allow practitioners to recover them now with the process of *soul retrieval*.

Shamanic practitioners use a trancelike state called the "shamanic journey" to bridge time and space. They locate the ages and reasons for soul loss and, with the permission of their client, retrieve these pieces. There are shamanic practitioners throughout the world who do this work. I have been assisting Gerry in recovering soul pieces through soul retrieval for 25 years. It can be done in person or remotely, such as through the telephone or Internet, so people can be helped worldwide. Gerry is now teaching others how to do it as well, because the need is so substantial.

~

Unfortunately, soul loss also causes certain beliefs to be ingrained into your unconscious belief systems. *Tessa Sayers,* who lives with the Turtle Mountain Band of Chippewa Indians in North Dakota, writes:

> *Everyone says when you change your beliefs, you change your life, so what is the best way to change those subconscious beliefs that seem very real? If you really believe something but would love to change it, how can you rework it into something better? For example, my belief that I should be able to overcome all my fears has*

created the unhealthy belief that I have failed if I can't overcome them. I put so much pressure on myself to "fix" these things (my fear of flying, staying alone, public speaking), the thought of not achieving that seems scary.

When you have a fear such as flying, speaking, or being alone, it may very well be related to soul loss. In this case, your inability to overcome a fear is not due to a failure on your part to manifest the change in your belief system. It is due to the brain's inability to write a new story, because it believes that it is protecting you by preserving your remaining soul energy. Your feeling of fear is actually your brain preventing you from doing something that it thinks could potentially lead to further loss of your power.

If you seek a shamanic practitioner to assist you through soul retrieval, your soul will fix the rest! Tiffany Nightingale shared a beautiful quote from noted anthropologist Alberto Villoldo that I feel really captures the work of soul retrieval: "The task of the shaman is to set free the energy bound in our stories, in our wounds, and to transform this energy into power and compassion within us, so that we may reclaim our own souls."

Please be gentle with yourself, and thank your brain for trying so hard to keep you safe. For it has not been doing this to hurt you, it has been doing it because it loves you and wishes to preserve your body.

～

Some people's paths lead them to help others manifest their greatness. They help people craft the story of their lives as well as the stories that their souls are looking to tell the world, in order to help still more people understand their stories! This is what **Christine Kloser,** "The Transformation Catalyst®" and founder of The Transformational Author Experience®, does. She has trained tens of thousands of aspiring authors to help them write, publish, and market their books through her live and online programs, which provide a way for emerging authors find their unique voice—and share it. Christine's work resonated with Gerry when he was ready to give up on writing, and so it is an honor to answer her question here:

What's the key to creating a life of overflowing abundance while enjoying a purposeful and prosperous career?

For many people there is a great divide between what you must do to earn a living and what you do to bring purpose to your life. Very often, this has to do with being raised with the concept that work is just that: *work.* But when you think back to the jobs that you aspired to as a child, weren't they the ones that appeared to be great fun? Many children describe wanting to be a doctor, fireman, policeman, dancer, musical star, or athlete—basically, any job filled with adventure and excitement that also contains some greater purpose. When you are young you are in touch with what your soul is calling out for: a form of work that will bring you joy!

Many have spoken to the relationship between abundance and career, such as in the memorable quote: "Do you what you love and the money will follow!" This is essentially true as long as your manifestation consciousness is not being overshadowed by your fear factor. Your "fear factor" is the level of energy you expend on wondering what you will do if the work you put into your passion and purpose does not pan out financially. If you spend a great deal of time thinking about this, then you are attracting a great deal of this energy to you. Fear is the great immobilizer and the direct opposite of the energy of faith and trust, so it will negate your manifestation energy if you give it too much importance.

Gerry let his fear factor take hold when he finished his first draft of *Messages from Margaret.* He hated what he'd written and began to wonder why he was doing this. He thought to himself: *The world already has authors who speak to angels, and even archangels. Who would really care about what Gerry Gavin from New Jersey and an angel named Margaret have to say? Besides, even if I did find somewhere to publish it, how would I ever manage to get the message out to the world?* So he put the manuscript aside, fairly certain that this was the end of the project.

With a little guidance from the angels, Gerry found Christine's Transformational Authors Program. Her course featured teachers who shared stories of when they were in the same place he was then, and this made him realize that he could succeed as well. Gerry was helped by not only the practical information he learned, but also the focus and motivation he regained. When he again trusted in himself, the angels, and the message, he drew to him the situations and people he needed.

If you are working but would like to transition into a different position, start looking at what tasks you already do that relate to your desired career. In this way, you begin to develop the skills you'll need so you can be ready when the opportunity manifests. For example, if you were a grade school teacher who desired to become a spiritual teacher, you'd become more mindful of the processes that help a child learn. If you were a manager who wanted to become a life coach, you could start taking note of which approaches best help your employees to work to their highest potential.

Always create abundance from the place where you are and don't wait for it to come from the place you are going. There are thousands every day who are transitioning into work that is more soul based, and that number will only grow as people become more attuned to their souls. What is of utmost concern is that you approach life with a burning desire. Desire is what makes things real. Desire is what makes you passionate about what you want in life. Desire is what motivates action and creativity. So when you are looking to manifest your joy, follow the path of that which you most desire!

CHAPTER
FIVE

YOUR BODY, HEALTH, AND CELLULAR MEMORY

> *"The most powerful healing techniques allow you to bring up and release cellular memories without dwelling on them."*

At this point, I hope I have explained the nature of your higher self and how you chose to incarnate for the purpose of expanding the energy of the soul. You might wonder, then, why you incarnate into a life form that starts out small and grows into maturity. Since you expand your soul's energy through your experiences, why not just incarnate into a fully adult human form and immediately start facing life's challenges? Well, the actual physical growth of the container that you have chosen is one of the ways that you grow the energy of the soul. You may begin as a seed or an egg, but as you expand from that form, you attract outside life-force energy to grow both physically and energetically.

So let us speak for a moment about the interrelation of the soul and the body, and what happens when you enter this physical form as a human being. *Lisbeth Hansen,* a garment maker and designer from Santa Rosa, California, asks:

At what point does the soul enter the body? Is it during conception, during the gestation, or just before birth?

This question so often comes up in your debates on Earth, and I hope to be able to explain this in as clear a manner as possible. It all begins with your higher self taking just a portion of its greater soul energy and making plans to place it within a new human being. When human life is created, the fetus grows within the mother as part of the mother's consciousness and part of the mother's physical energy. A human's life force is constantly reinforced by taking in energy around you through your breath; as a fetus, however, you do not breathe. Your mother is breathing for you and bringing in life force to allow you to grow.

During this time period, your brain and body are recording memories within your growing cellular structure—but you are not yet you! At various times you will familiarize yourself with the energy of your mother and your new form by sending your soul energy in and out through your mother's solar plexus chakra, but you do not take up permanent residence immediately. You are just getting used to the restrictions that this physical form will impose and trying to figure out how much of your soul energy will be needed to support this new life form. Your mother is generally aware of these fleeting, sporadic times and will feel you as a unique being. This testing of the physical container grows more frequent in the final weeks of pregnancy, and it happens daily in the last few days before birth, as your higher self assesses the exact amount of energy that will be required for the baby's life support.

Then, as you take your first breath into your body at birth, you draw in your unique soul energy. This is the moment that you and your mother become separate unique conscious energies. Your brain and body retain the cellular memories of your fetal experience, which is why many people who have experienced past-life regression assume that their soul was present at the fetal period. However, you are not a true individual being until the moment of the first separate breath from the mother.

❧

This body you inhabit has a very sophisticated communication system to keep you in optimal health. Every day your body speaks to you and lets you know how your actions are affecting its well-being. It may speak to you with heartburn after you have eaten a certain type of food, or cravings for carbohydrates after a strenuous workout. But the most noticeable communication of the body is when it is speaking to you through *pain*. Pain is the body's way of telling you that something is out of balance. There may be an injury in the area, or the discomfort may be a side effect of the body's healing process. Often, however, pain is the result of cellular memory that is trying to get your attention!

If you have not heard of cellular memory, let me explain it in as simple terms as possible. Your body, this earth, and the entire universe are made up of cells. Within the structure of your body, every memory that you have—from the time that you were first conceived and in the womb of your mother to your final memory at the time of your death—is stored within your body and aura, the energetic area around your body. However, to understand the concept of cellular memory more clearly, I must first explain to you the relationship between your soul and your brain.

When you are maturing as a fetus, your brain grows in size and operating capacity as it replicates all of the components of your parents' brains. The collective souls upgrade the conscious energy of the individual soul, so as you have been evolving as a race, you pass on more and more of your collective knowledge to each new generation. This is why a 3-year-old has the capacity to operate technology that baffles his 80-year-old grandfather. Young ones are literally hardwired to be more in touch, to understanding many functions that they just seem to "know."

As you are born and your body matures, your brain continues to store its memories, usually as complete cells that contain both the cognitive memory (the memory of what occurred) and the emotional memory (the memory of the emotions evoked by that event). The brain's primary function is to keep the body in a state of balance, so when something upsets that balance, the brain attempts to minimize damage by splitting the cellular memory of this event so that the cells containing the emotional memory are stored in one part of the body, while the cells containing the cognitive memory are stored in another. (The other way that your body tries to protect you from trauma is through soul loss, as we discussed previously.)

Although this process protects you in the short run, it creates unusual cell structures. The cells get stored deep in tissue or muscle, usually in places where you are unlikely to physically touch it, such as deep in the abdominal wall or behind the shoulder blades. However, because like energy attracts like energy, when you encounter similar emotional situations in your life, these new memory cells will split and attach to similar cells, which split and reproduce just as all other cells do. These "hidden" cells do not fit in with the structure of the other cells in the region where they are stored, as they are not complete cells, and often your body will alert you to this through the sensation of pain.

Think for a moment of the emotional experiences in your life. Perhaps your parents divorce when you are small, and your father, whom you love dearly, moves out of the house. The overwhelming emotion of this abandonment causes your brain to split the cells of your cognitive memory and the emotional memory in an effort to help control your physical and emotional pain. Then, years later, your high school sweetheart breaks up with you in favor of your best friend. Your brain recognizes this energy of abandonment, so when it splits the memory, it stores the cells in the same places where it stored the memory of your father leaving you. Tragedy strikes again years later when your father, who has been your closest friend and supporter throughout your life, dies in a car accident. Although you logically know that this situation is different, as your father did not choose to leave you, your body feels the energy of it as the same. The overwhelming emotion from this event brings attention to the stored cellular memory, which causes your body to call out through physical pain or anxiety, as it desires to release this energy that is providing no positive function for the body. Although the discomfort may be slight at first, your body's calls will get louder and louder if you try to ignore it or sedate it with medication. Cellular memory is often what is at the core of many physical illnesses.

One method to help people release cellular memory that may be causing them pain, anxiety, and physical or emotional illness is "tapping," which is also known as the Emotional Freedom Techniques (EFT). A pioneer in the field, **Nick Ortner,** created a documentary and wrote a *New York Times* best-selling book on this amazing modality, both called *The Tapping Solution.* Years ago, Gerry purchased the documentary, loved it, and began utilizing this effective technique himself. At the time, Gerry had just become the publisher of a community newspaper group in New York City, where Nick lived, so he had a reporter interview Nick for his "Alternative Healthy Manhattan" section. What neither of them knew at the time was that just a few short years later they would both be authors for Hay House—and soft-spoken Nick would become the worldwide voice for tapping!

Always looking to learn more about the healing process, Nick shares the following question:

Is it important to clean up the past, or should we just focus on a positive future and ignore the past?

In short, the answer to your question is *yes.* Yes, it is important to clean up energy that you are holding on to from the past, and yes, it is also important to let that energy go and focus on a positive future! While that might seem confusing, let me explain.

The brain stores cellular memory throughout the body, which can be the cause of physical discomfort, so it stands to reason that ridding yourself of that energy is important to your physical health. But sometimes human beings are overly focused on the difficulties of their past experiences and use it as a justification for their current health or the nature of the lives that they are living. This leads them to miss out on possibilities for healing and the potential for joy day in and day out, which they would see if they were living in the present.

When part of you is focused on your negative life experiences, it is difficult to make loving and compassionate decisions about your current situation to allow you to increase your vibration. The most productive action is to recognize that while your past may have created some of your current situation, your true power—your ability to harness energy around you—is always in the present moment. You can release old, negative patterns with self-love rather than regret or resentment, because you are grateful that they have taught you so much! That is why the most powerful healing techniques allow you to bring up and release cellular memories without dwelling on them. Lingering on painful memories creates emotional energy that attracts more of the same energy into your life.

Tapping is a wonderful form of energy work that you can do on yourself. It works on the meridians of the body and utilizes the power of the throat chakra to allow you to give voice to your frustrations while still acknowledging and honoring that you love, appreciate, and accept yourself as you are. Essentially you are in the present moment and having a conversation with your body in which you are listening to and speaking out loud about your pain while tapping on acupressure points on your body's meridians that interconnect with every part of your central nervous system—thus connecting with and releasing the energy.

Sometimes tapping serves to uncover what the pain is actually hiding. One of the most moving scenes in *The Tapping Solution* documentary takes place when a Vietnam veteran discovers that the source of the debilitating back pain that has plagued him for years—which has not improved despite all types of therapies, surgeries, and medications—is actually the buried painful memories of wartime. He is pain-free after using tapping to communicate with his pain and release these memories, and he remains pain-free to this day. His life is also filled with more joy and better relationships because he has released the guilt of his wartime actions.

Not to be critical of other types of talk therapies, but sometimes a person can find themselves stuck in the emotions of the past if they are brought up without being coupled with techniques to release the energy of those memories. You cannot create energy in thoughts of your past. No amount of regret or grief will ever change a situation that has already happened. This is why it is powerfully healing to focus not so much on a positive future but on a positive *present!*

This is not to say that you shouldn't have goals, aspirations, or dreams for the future, as that is what provides motivation for your present-day actions and thoughts. However, no manner of positive thoughts about your future will produce a manifesting effect if you are not allowing that same positive thought pattern to encircle your present thoughts. Again, the present is the only place in your life where you are energetically powerful.

⁓

When Nick Ortner decided to make *The Tapping Solution* movie, he trusted his heart and intuition to guide him and asked his sister, **Jessica Ortner,** to lead the interviews. Her genuineness, joyfulness, and sincerity came through in the film as well as the subsequent interviews she has conducted for the annual Tapping World Summits. She combined these qualities with frank honesty about her struggles with self-image to write *The Tapping Solution for Weight Loss & Body Confidence.* The subject of body image continues in her question:

How does one create a loving and supportive relationship with their body if they feel that their body is betraying them, due to an illness or struggles with their weight? And why is it so important to love your body in its current state?

Humankind often tends not to create cooperative relationships, whether it's with things outside of themselves—such as this planet and the other people, animals, and natural resources on it—or, for that matter, things inside of themselves! Many people, for example, take their body and health very much for granted. When you are in a relationship that you take for granted and something you feel entitled to unexpectedly changes, you somehow feel betrayed.

I would like to use a story to illustrate why this feeling of betrayal is somewhat misguided. Imagine for a moment that you are a self-centered person in a relationship. You really don't pay a lot of attention to your partner, and he has just accepted a very lucrative position in another country. (I use this example to somewhat illustrate an "out of sight, out of mind" relationship.) So, like clockwork, he sends you money while asking for nothing in return.

In the beginning you are so happy and excitedly spend the extra income, enjoying all it brings and feeling very grateful for the source. But soon, because of your self-centered nature, you come to take the money for granted. You don't feel the need to communicate with your partner, the source of your well-being. In fact, you acknowledge him only when he complains about something. As his complaints get louder, you begin to look for solutions to shut him up. Then one day the checks begin to slow down, and in turn you have to adjust your lifestyle; but you are more concerned with having things go back to normal rather than what your partner is trying to say to you about his needs. Finally, your partner's exhaustion and stress causes him to lose the ability to do his job, and you feel betrayed. "How could you do this to me?" you ask him. "You have a responsibility to me! I count on you, and you are letting me down! Why can't you get back to work the way you did before?"

But no matter how much your partner loves you, he cannot repair the damage by himself. Now you are forced to focus on the relationship and your partner's needs. You may seek the perspective of an expert—perhaps a doctor of some sort—to suggest ways to heal the damage and help build a healthy new relationship. You are taught the importance of loving your partner not for the things he can do for you, but rather just because he is your partner and you truly appreciate *everything* about him—and you are in this together!

Just as in the story, humans become very used to relying on their body because it is designed to do so much without you having to give it much thought. It is very easy to take your body's health and energy for granted, allowing it to consistently offer you service no matter how much you ignore its needs. The body adapts to everything you can throw at it, while trying to draw attention to its needs through anxiety and pain. When the complaints of the body go unheeded, then the body is forced to ramp up its complaining. But people generally find methods (medicine) to mask the noise of the pain without ever really *talking* to your body to ask: "Why are you in pain?"

After too much neglect of its needs, the body can no longer work for you like it did in the past. This is often when you come to the perspective that your body is betraying you, as it goes through illness or weight struggles. You've assumed for so long that you can depend on your body as one of the most constant and dependable parts of your life. But your body needs to be able to depend on you to listen to it as well. The two human functions that bring forth the greatest amount of attention are sex and eating, as both are so heavily associated with pleasure and, although you might not realize it, self-love.

This leads to the second part of the question: "Why is it so important to love your body in its current state?" The reason is that your body has reached its current state due to its perceptions of what is the best possible way to love you—to protect you and fulfill your needs and desires! For example, even when cellular memory from traumatic experiences is causing you pain, this stems from your brain trying to protect your mental well-being through sequestering these memories in various parts of your body.

Sometimes the body will even build up a cushion of protection to prevent you from somehow accidentally touching upon these memories. It places deposits of fat and tissue around areas with trapped cellular memory, which is often in the abdomen, although it can be in any area. Your attempts to remove this weight may be thwarted by your body slowing down your metabolism or another means because it is still trying to protect you from these memories.

So while your brain and body might be working together to take actions that they think are loving toward you, you might be unhappy and defer loving your current form until you are healthy or thin. The more emphasis you put on some future occurrence as being necessary to love your body, the longer it takes to actually reach that state. When there is no present level of gratitude for what you have, you can't attract more of what you desire. And if you are signaling to your body with your thinking that your body is fat or sick, then your body will respond with more of the same. Once you accept that your current condition and everything you experience began because your body saw this as a way to protect you and make you happy, then you can begin to love the body you are in. In doing so, you are thanking your body for all it has done to protect you in the past and allowing it to slowly evolve with you.

So give thanks for your current body and appreciate it for all its work! Ask it *how* to best listen to it and interpret its signals when it is speaking to you. It greatly helps to do mirror work; look in the mirror and say to yourself, "I love you. I love you now with no conditions. I make it my heart's work to learn to love you as much as you have loved me!"

You cannot wait to love yourself until you meet some future condition. Think of the love that you give to a child; this is the basis of how you should love yourselves at all stages of your lives. You do not say to a baby, "I will love you when you learn to talk" or "I won't love you until you learn to walk." You would not think that this baby is not worthy until it no longer needs its diaper changed. Every stage of learning and need is part of the evolution of the human body. You love your baby through every stage of the human growth process; don't suddenly withhold that acceptance for all aspects of yourself at adulthood. Conditional love is at the root of all weight and health issues.

∽

Even after they've accepted their body for its current condition, many still wonder what makes some people more predisposed to illness than others. *Michelle Edinburg,* an art therapist from Solihull, England, notes a distinction in types of disease:

> *How are hereditary illnesses different from diseases that manifest later in life, and can they be healed in a person's lifetime?*

It is true that there is a difference between illnesses that are hereditary and those that occur due to other factors. Hereditary conditions can be inherited from the belief systems and health habits of your ancestors, but your predisposition to their manifestation also depends on your own beliefs and the care you take of your body. Diseases that develop later in life, on the other hand, have a direct relationship to factors such as your personal lifestyle, beliefs, and stress.

Hereditary diseases are thought forms that are passed from parent to child. Just as the brain retains memories from the fetal experience even though the soul has not yet entered, the fetus also retains in-womb experiences expressed by the mother as well as the most extreme emotions that form part of the consciousness of the father. So if a mother is calm and joyful, then it is likely the baby will fall into similar patterns. If the mother has a concern about a genetic disorder, then it is likely that this thought will permeate her pregnancy unless it is tempered by thoughts of the baby being born healthy; this adds to the likelihood of the genetic markings of the disease becoming dominant.

Dominant is an important word when we are speaking about thought forms, as your brain will recognize your most dominant thought. The genetic structure of your ancestors may have been changed by repressed cellular memories, causing certain genes to be passed down through your family. However, a predisposition to a hereditary illness only means that someone before you in your bloodline had that disease. There are many other traits in life that your family can cause you to be predisposed to, such as being a drug addict, or a pedophile, or a shopaholic. Just because there are people in your bloodline who have experienced such things, that does not mean that *you* have to acquire this condition as well. Although scientists might make predictions as to the likelihood of something occurring, this can spread fear and cause a condition to become a dominant thought.

So yes, dear ones, it is possible for a hereditary condition to be changed by a single individual within a bloodline who focuses on thoughts of well-being. A pregnant mother who believes in the complete health of her fetus will go a long way toward giving that child the predisposition toward health. However, I want to make it clear here that I am not trying to place undue stress on mothers. I am not saying your thoughts during your pregnancy are the only things that affect hereditary conditions. Of course there are some mothers who think nothing but positive and healthy thoughts during a pregnancy, yet deliver a child with complications or a hereditary condition that no one in the family was aware of.

Sometimes the decision to take on a health challenge can actually be the decision of the incarnating soul for the experience of soul growth for all parties involved. My intent here is just to help you feel empowered by your thoughts rather than hopeless over something you see as "inevitable."

I recall a wonderful bumper sticker that I think brings a bit of lightness to this situation. It read, "Insanity is hereditary—you get it from your kids!" In no way do I want make fun of anyone's struggle with a genetic disease. I simply wish to emphasize the necessity of focusing on what is strong and solid in the world rather than on what is broken and discordant. The more you focus on the things that bring you joy, that which brings *ease* to your life, then the less likely you are to develop *dis-ease*. In other words, that which puts your body at less ease can cause other problems as well.

For example, I often speak to women during readings who are very concerned because they are unable to get pregnant and have found no medical reason as to why. Nearly all of these particular women describe feeling like they are up against the "biological clock," referring to that man-made deadline for getting pregnant. Panic sets in as men and women worry about the complications of later-age pregnancy and of losing their chance to ever have a baby. They develop a repetitive thought form that speaks to birth defects and getting too old, and their brains instruct the body to avoid that dangerous situation by not allowing the woman to become pregnant.

In contrast to the biological clock, you might recall "change of life" babies. These are babies born to couples who think they can no longer have children because the woman is older and in the early stages of menopause, so they've been having fun, unworried sex, much like they did in their youth.

So this is what I often advise couples who are struggling: Go back to the things you used to do before you worried about getting pregnant. Act like two giddy teenagers and make love with reckless abandon. Forget the schedules and temperature charts! The less fear you have around pregnancy, the more you increase your chances of becoming pregnant and having a healthy baby—regardless of the "clock"!

≈

Some diseases have their root not in the communication system of your thoughts with your body but with the body's communication between its own systems. *Dr. Kristen Willeumier*, a neuroscientist from Los Angeles, California, studies two of these diseases, which are very similar in their makeup. She asks:

Could you please explain what happens to the brain in neuro-degenerative disease processes like Alzheimer's and Parkinson's? Do you have any recommendations as to how to proactively prevent these health issues? We have found that Alzheimer's starts 30 years before the onset of symptoms, so angelic wisdom as to how to maintain our highest functioning brains would be greatly appreciated. If it is true that disease occurs when we move away from Spirit, as said in <u>A Course in Miracles</u>, how can we be more aware of this process so we can help ourselves get back on track?

First of all, I wish to thank you for your courage, Kristen, in looking at disease from not only the physical and scientific level but also the soul level. Indigenous shamans believed that illness came from something going out of balance within a person, the world around them, or a person's connection with their soul. When you realize that your soul is *in* all of those things, it becomes clear that a strong connection to your soul is what will help you understand how to take greater care of the other pieces.

Alzheimer's disease and Parkinson's disease are degenerative malfunctions of the communication systems within the human body. It is true that you can study and see some of the processes of these diseases in the brain, but they are also taking place in the gut as well as in the enteric nervous system. Most people are not aware that there are five times as many neurons that run from your throat all the way to your anus as are located in your spinal cord. That is amazing in scope because there are well over 100 million neurons traveling through the spinal cord! As part of the enteric nervous system, these neurons are responsible for reflexes and decisive thought functions, and they are subject to substantive degenerative damage as the result of prolonged neurological chemical production caused by stress responses. To understand the progress of these diseases, we first need to discuss how your physical body interacts with the energy in your chakra system.

Your chakra system regulates the energy that is coming into your body much like the circuit breakers in your homes. You have seven chakras, which are, from top to bottom: crown, third eye, throat, heart, solar plexus, sacral, and root. Energy comes into your body from three directions. The first direction is energy that enters the crown chakra at the top of your head, which comes from your connection to your higher self. This energy travels down from the crown to the forehead area through the third eye chakra, which processes your logical and intuitive thoughts and regulates all the physical energy for the head region. The energy then progresses to your throat chakra, where you have the ability to create a vibration frequency to communicate—what you call your "voice." This chakra controls the physical functions of the throat, shoulders, and arms, and it is the gatekeeper of the emotions and the beginnings of your enteric nervous system. The energy then continues to your heart chakra, which controls your emotions and the physical functions of your heart, lungs, and gallbladder.

The second direction of energy comes from the direction of the earth. Your body draws energy up into you that helps communicate the things you need to do to keep your body alive and to create more life. The first chakra that energy enters into is the root chakra at the base of the spine, which sends energy to the central nervous system as well as the enteric nervous system. This chakra regulates your survival skills, so this chakra assists in the end of your digestive process and also offers energy to your legs in the fight-or-flight stress response. The energy then moves up to the area just above your sexual organs to the sacral chakra, which regulates all of the energy for your sexual and reproductive responses, part of your digestive responses, and your creative energy.

Finally, the energy that is traveling up from the earth and the energy that is coming down from your higher self meet right at your solar plexus chakra. This chakra is at the heart of the functions of your enteric nervous system. It puts together all of the information it receives from both directions and adds it to the information it is pulling in from your relationship to other human beings. Your solar plexus chakra is constantly sharing energy with others through what you might know as sympathetic energy exchange. This is where your cognitive understanding of another person's energy causes you to respond to them in a certain way. This chakra also regulates your empathetic response center, which allows you to actually "feel" another person's energy.

The solar plexus chakra is your power center because not only are you sharing power and understanding here but also creating your physical responses to the energy that is being sent through your system. When your chakras are clear and the information they are sending is unfettered, this region can make strong "gut" decisions that allow you to take decisive action. You will feel it if this chakra becomes damaged because the energy regulating your stress response will become impaired and cause dysfunction to the central nervous system, affecting your reflexes and ability to produce short-term memory.

Much disease is affected by the energy (food) that humans ingest and the way that humans physically respond to stress. As your societal evolution has moved from prioritizing physical activity to mental activity, the effects of stress become more pronounced. When the stress response is activated, the central nervous system and enteric nervous system converse through the throat chakra, and chemical signals are produced to strengthen the muscles, heighten awareness, and create fast reflexes. When you react to a physical danger, then this energy can be expended in fight or flight. But when your stressors are emotional or mental, then your body has no physical outlet to release this energy. This can cause tensed muscles to harden (arthritis), nerve blockage and resulting referred pain (fibromyalgia), exhaustion of the adrenal glands from producing constant adrenaline (adrenal fatigue), and short-circuiting of the central nervous system, which results in inconsistent and involuntary communication/reflex response (Tourette's and early Parkinson's) and degenerative muscle and tissue response (later-stage Parkinson's).

In the case of Alzheimer's disease, there is a block in communication between the enteric and central nervous systems. This occurs as a result of the stress response as well, but it is more directly related to cellular memory buried within the tissue of the enteric nervous system. The brain does not want the cellular memory of this traumatic event to come to the surface, so it begins to cut off communication with the enteric system. This short circuit allows the person to have very clear access to most cognitive memories of the past, but it becomes difficult to create or store short-term memory. The new memory cells essentially are unable to form, and they scatter and become attached to other parts of the body, hastening their degeneration. The person with Alzheimer's is stuck in a "loop" of cognitive experiences, not realizing that they are repeatedly saying or thinking the same thing. Anger and paranoia tends to come to the surface as their survival instincts call to mind past dangers, and they often misdirect the source of this danger as coming from those around them.

Another predisposition, if you will, for Alzheimer's disease is having an extremely empathetic nature. When you are empathetic, you draw energy into your body that your brain is unable to separate from your own thought forms or feelings, and it stores them in your cellular memory as your own.

Now as to maintaining your physical, mental, and energetic health, the truth is not really as complicated as you might think. I have often been accused of offering solutions that seem far too simple to actually be effective—and I am afraid that this is going to be one of those times! The following are simple things that you can do to substantially improve your physical health and will provide you with increased energy and joy.

— **Exercise:** Your physical body was not designed to be still. It was designed to be a vessel for your soul to experience all types of things. For that reason you have been given the ability to run, stretch, jump, swim, twirl, dance, climb, cycle, have sex, and do so very many other things. You were created to expend energy, and when you were a child you understood this clearly as you climbed trees, played sports, ran, jumped, and played with your friends. Indeed, one of the dangers of the electronic age is that many children are more content to play a video game of a sport than to play the sport themselves. Fun and playful exercise needs to be nurtured in children.

As you age you become more serious and lose your desire to play. You spend your time sitting in an office, sitting in a restaurant, sitting on a couch, then lying down in bed before starting over again the next day. Many of those who exercise do so because they have to rather than because it is fun. When the joy is removed from exercise, you lose a part of the regenerative and relaxing nature of it. It might be raising your heart rate, but it is not raising your *vibration*.

Exercise in ways that are fun to you. Pick up a sport you played as a kid and play by yourself or with a friend. If you love to walk, do so, but pick up the pace a little bit and maybe even make a game of it. If you would like to do an activity that you used to do as a kid and have no one to do it with, then volunteer at a kids' program. Organizations are always looking for volunteers to work with youth, and you can share your skills with those who will appreciate it.

Do not worry about being a "grown-up." Your desire is to release stress from your body, and there is no faster way to release stress than to experience joy! Coupling joy with your exercise will create a profound change in your body as well as your mental outlook and energy.

— **Meditate:** I know that I am now totally confusing you because I just suggested that you be more active and now I am telling you to sit quietly in stillness! But combining exercise with quiet times of meditation will not only double the effectiveness of stress relief but also set you up to actually be less receptive to stress.

Stress is not a condition but a reaction! It is how you are choosing to respond to a given situation. When you feel stress from worry, it is essentially creating a stress response to potential conditions that have not even happened!

One of the best tools for regulating your stress response is to meditate every day. Meditation is so important because it allows you to focus on your breath as it carries energy in and out of your body. Remember that breath carries life-force energy; the more time you focus on just your breath, the more energy you bring into your body and the more stress you breathe out.

If you have a minute, then you have time to meditate with Gerry's very simple breathing technique. All you have to do is close your eyes and breathe in, counting slowly to seven in your mind. Then you hold your breath for a count of seven, and exhale for a count of seven. Repeat these steps three more times.

After just a minute, you will feel a tremendous difference in the tension in your body. If you continue to do it for five minutes, you will feel amazing. This technique works because the mind can focus on only one thought at a time. If you are focused on your breathing and counting, then your mind is as well.

By the way, Gerry named this the "Lucky 7" technique because the three counts of seven made him think of a slot machine at a casino. He felt like this simple meditation was like hitting the stress-relief jackpot!

— **Be Mindful of Your Food:** The food available from the earth is there to help you have a healthy life and support your immune and nervous systems. But the enteric nervous system in particular is damaged by food that is filled with chemical preservatives. Your body will do its best to digest these foods, but the food stabilizers are active not only on the shelf but also in your intestines. Your digestive acids are unable to fully extract nutrients and energy, and the result leaves you feeling sluggish and foggy.

The other problem is that the diet of most humans is very acidic when it should be more alkaline. When the balance of your system is toward the acidic, healthy bacteria are killed while unhealthy bacteria proliferate. This leaves you vulnerable to all types of illness, including cancer. No illness or infections from unhealthy bacteria can live in an alkaline environment. Higher levels of alkalinity in your body increase your ability to create a healthy physical environment. Eating mostly live foods, such as fruits and vegetables, supports an alkaline balance in the body. Juicing can help a highly acidic body absorb the alkaline food better.

Please also make sure that your food does not contain genetically modified organisms (GMOs)! Corporations have modified the natural cellular structure of the food in dangerous ways in order to grow and sell more food. Unnatural substances such as GMOs will eventually create disease in an area of the digestive tract. If you desire to eat meat, please make sure that it is organic and antibiotic-free, and that the animal has not been fed grain that contains pesticides, preservatives, or GMOs. Also, please try to find animals who have been raised with honor and respect and whose life is taken without fearful trauma. You become what you eat, and they have become what they ate and what they experience!

The key, dear ones, is to work toward a revolution in your food industry. It is crucial that you move back to an organic and non-chemical-infused diet. Food is the biggest cause of the damage to your enteric nervous system and is therefore the biggest cause of disease—second only to stress. But the effects of stress are amplified by the effects of food.

— **Release Cellular Memory:** We've spoken in this chapter about all of the physical conditions that can be caused or compounded by cellular memory. The wonderful thing is that these memories can be easily released. I would urge everyone reading this book to please learn about tapping (EFT). It is something that you can do to help yourself as well as your family. Imagine your children being able to release unwanted cellular memory as soon as they start to record it!

Other techniques will help as well. Massage helps release memory stored in surface-level muscles and tissues. Myofascial release goes a little deeper to release memory in the fascia that underlies your tissues, muscles, and organs. Reiki is extremely effective in harnessing the power of life force that is all around you to activate your body's innate knowledge of how to heal. You can receive Reiki from a practitioner or learn Reiki level one to perform it on yourself and others.

If you feel yourself being called to a different type of energy or bodywork, then please trust your intuition. Your consciousness and your body are constantly trying to guide you to release what is not in your best interest. Listen to your body's messages. Do not ever ignore persistent pain, dear ones, as that is your body trying to get your attention. If you take the time to communicate with your body, it will always let you know what it needs—and it won't need to shout it out with pain!

— **Reclaim Your Power and Your Soul:** In the previous chapter I described soul loss and explained the physical conditions that it may cause. You may be able to identify it in yourself by considering some simple questions: Do you feel that you are just not yourself? Does it feel like something is missing? Do you think to yourself, *I have just not been the same since . . . ?* The event could be the death of a loved one, the loss of a job, an operation, a romantic breakup, or something you can't identify. If you feel called toward soul retrieval, please contact Gerry through his website at www.gerrygavin.com for more information so you can more deeply understand and correct it. It is a very simple, very gentle, very joyful, and very powerful process.

While all of these things are well within your power, it can be hard to change established behaviors. Each of you will likely come from a different place. For example, tapping might help change your food cravings, so it would be a good place to start before trying to change your diet. Or you may want to experience soul retrieval so you can be fully present energetically for your other tasks. Maybe you already eat well but need to find a fun way to exercise. If you need support to get going and can't find any,

I would suggest finding a group or starting your own through a website such as www.meetup.com.

Your higher self and, of course, your angels are here to help you! Just feel free to ask. Remember that although you are living in a material (physical) world, this is only a small part of you. You can always access the bigger part for help.

IT'S ALL RELATIVE

The Truth about Relationships

> *"Love isn't perfect. Love is complicated.*
> *Love doesn't work exactly as you would like*
> *it to work. Love is messy!"*

A major portion of your energy is taken up with interactions with other people, and this energetic interaction is channeled through your solar plexus chakra. Your relationships with others in this world fall into five basic categories: family, friends, romantic relationships, work associates, and people who share like interests. Each of these relationships is a measure by which you define your-self as a person, and each will either raise or diminish your energetic vibration. You open your heart and your energetic being to others through relationships, which is why most of your damaging cellular memory and soul loss happens as a result of these interactions. You can exchange love, which is energy, and you can also cause others to experience the pain of your disapproval or lack of love!

Gerry noticed a common sentiment about love while watching a Valentine's Day marathon on Hallmark TV, which he is a big fan of. (He loves uplifting movies, is an incurable romantic, and really enjoys happy endings.) Many movies had a character say something like: "Love isn't perfect," "Love is complicated," "Love doesn't work exactly as you would like it to work," and "Love is messy!" Gerry thought of how love is demonstrated by billions of individual people, each of whom has their own interpretation and way of expressing it because of their unique experiences.

Each of you is the lead character in this story of your life, and you play that lead like no one else. Someone might say you are just like your mom or dad, but I guarantee that you are not. There is always something different in your interpretation of life, however slight it might be. Your love as a parent is not the same as your parents' love, and your love for your children will be different from your children's love for theirs.

Mike Dooley, the *New York Times* best-selling author of *Infinite Possibilities* and *The Top Ten Things Dead People Want to Tell YOU*, starts our conversation about relationships with a deeply personal question:

> *Most of us know that we choose our lives and the parents we'll have, and our parents must choose or agree to us. I am a first-time dad, so can you speak to this process of choosing, from both the baby's and parents' perspectives?*

You are correct that in your soul state you do choose the parents to whom you will be born, and those souls who will be your parents are also involved in the selection process. I love that your question is rooted in the deeply personal nature of your being a first-time father and wondering how this perspective then works in your life. Here it is in a nutshell!

Every soul desires to have experiences in a physical form that allow them opportunities to expand their energy. So you choose circumstances, including your parents, in consideration of their potential for energetic, or spiritual, growth. Some parents are chosen to be a loving support for this growth, while others are chosen to be a challenge to this growth in order to spur you to seek it on your own. You might understand that the struggles in your personal life offered you tremendous opportunities for self-realization and growth. As a new father, however, you seek to offer your child as loving and protected an environment as you can create. Although it is natural to want to pass on the opportunities and wisdom that you have gleaned over your lifetime, it is very likely that your child will make the decision to follow a different path from yours in order to experience their personal growth.

There is an old adage that people never appreciate the wisdom of their parents until they become a mom or dad themselves. This is because when you take on your human form, you are no longer aware of the soul plan that you made as your higher self. Everything from the point of physical creation (birth) is pure improvisation. So while your child might make the decision to be born into a family that offers all the advantages of a "jump-started" spiritual life, it is not a guarantee that they will recognize this potential and take advantage of it. It is so important for all parents to remember that all you can do is invite your child to learn from your experiences, as their path may take them in very different directions. However, one of the best ways a parent can share knowledge is to create delightful experiences that the child will connect with the lesson. Above all the soul seeks to experience joy, so if you make that the root of the teaching, then the student embraces the experience and accepts it as truth.

Mike, in this lifetime you are experiencing the energy of being a teacher. It is not something that you originally thought you would be doing, but circumstances have brought you to this place where you feel a strong desire to share what you have learned. Much of what you teach are those things that you yourself once desired or needed to learn. When you help your child with learning, you also help your own teaching. Furthermore, you will be helping your child with learning those things that they will teach in the future as well! That is why parents, if they are open, can learn as much from their children as their children do from them!

The most critical lesson that parents can impart to their child is to seek joy in their lives! If they can learn this in their formative years, many other lessons that are encompassed within this concept will be learned as well. As much as possible, limit the lessons that impart fear. Let your children explore their curiosity; pull them in only when there is clear and present danger. Children are often taught to fear things that are unlikely to ever happen, which only produces a predisposition for anxiety rather than safety. If you learn to see the joy in all things, then all things will bring you joy!

∾

It is important to note here that the process of soul loss and damaging cellular memory begins when you are just a child. At a very young age, you learn of the enjoyment you receive when you bring pleasure to other people. When a baby falls while first learning to walk, they may see a laughing mommy and daddy say, "You fall down; go boom!" The child is thrilled that their action has brought about such a joyful reaction and sets out to do it over and over again. But as that child grows older, they begin to learn that the laughter and approval of a parent is now based on their meeting certain expectations of behavior! They must act a certain way, perform well in school, and interact with friends and family just so. Finally, the education system will replace students' individuality with a set of collected beliefs and approved ways of processing knowledge. Imagination gets left to younger years, and playfulness gets more and more discouraged every year.

I assist Gerry with soul-retrieval work, and every week he brings back soul pieces from clients' childhoods. We see preschool and elementary-school pieces from when they felt powerless and unable to live up to their parents' expectations and teenage pieces who were criticized by teachers for being lazy or told that they would never amount to anything! These hurts are magnified as an adult when you find yourself attracting the same pattern. The love you seek has conditions attached; and when someone offers you conditional love, you tend to do the same. Your ability to offer love to another becomes contingent on their doing certain things or being a certain way first. But that just isn't how energy—or love—works! It is subject to the same principle as everything else—the law of attraction.

The law of attraction led **Arielle Ford** to her path as a publicist and producer who has helped launch the careers of numerous great teachers in the New Thought movement. However, it wasn't until she decided to apply those same laws to her personal sphere that she found the love of her life. She shared this story in *The Soulmate Secret,* which became an international bestseller, and followed this up with relationship wisdom in *Wabi Sabi Love.* She asks:

How and why is it important for couples to "choose love" even when they are "not feeling it"?

This question is so very important for the understanding of "couple" relationships. When a person decides to choose love, even when they do not feel it or may not want to at the time, it allows for some urgent energetic shifts to take place.

First, choosing love means that you are coming from a place of heartfelt caring and compassion. At the beginning of a relationship, people feel excitement, passion, and connection, which bring them a strong sense of love and belonging. Over time, however, that initial attraction and loving passion wane. The collective attention of the couple begins to dwarf the individual needs of each person in their "day in, day out" existence. Stress accumulates and dulls those initial feelings of love as each person begins to associate their partner with their relationship problems rather than what was their joint passion. This causes couples to no longer "feel" love the way they did in the beginning.

By choosing love, an individual makes a conscious decision to focus on those feelings and thoughts that had initially brought them joy in the relationship. For example, when you fall in love, how the other person feels is of utmost importance to you. You spend time trying to get to know them, listening with interest and care. You try to do things just to see a smile on your partner's face because their happiness brings joy into your own life—and that elevates your energy! But what you may not have realized is that what truly elevated your energy was not what you were doing for that other person, but rather the energy of love that you were bringing up within yourself!

When you love, you put yourself into the flow of the very essence of your being, your soul. In so doing, you raise your own vibration, and you feel a sense of euphoria and elevated well-being. This is the true secret of love: when you love another person, the feelings you experience are not about the energy that person directs toward you but rather the energy that is being created by you! You feel a sense of well-being because you are creating a loving energy within yourself and expanding that energy outward.

That is why choosing love is so important. When you are not feeling love, it is easy to draw forth other emotions like resentment, anger, frustration—even hatred. You send the energy of whatever you are feeling out into the universe, and the result is that you attract to you more of the same type of energy. That is why people who are having conflicts in one relationship often find that this energy extends into other relationships in their life. So when you are feeling anger with your partner, you are literally creating a field of that energy around you, and that energy is acting like a magnet to attract more of the same. By electing to choose love, you dissipate that energy and allow yourself to be surrounded by a loving compassionate energy instead.

This may seem like a difficult thing to do at first, but choosing love is simply about bringing to the forefront of your consciousness all the best qualities of the other person. In other words, you are remembering what caused you to fall in love in the first place. Even if your partner isn't exhibiting these behaviors in the present, your memories allow you to recall the experiences and feelings that caused your initial attraction. It puts you back in the emotional charge that you felt at that time so you can reawaken these internal feelings in yourself. You're remembering what makes you feel loved and what makes you feel "in love." You may notice that your heart center begins to soften, and you find yourself moving out of anger, resentment, or remorse and moving into a state of forgiveness for both yourself and your partner.

Many couples reach a point in their relationship where they find themselves questioning why they are with their partner in the first place. But few actually take the time to go back and consider the true reasons for why they did fall in love, because they are so full of other emotions. They might even believe that thinking or acting in a loving manner is being weak and giving away their power. But love and compassion are the greatest powers in the universe; you can never give away your power by practicing them!

When you choose love you bring forward the energy of love to you! That energy then surrounds you and attracts more love to you. If you find it hard for your brain to allow you to produce loving thoughts, then ask yourself the question, "Why is it so easy for me to love my partner?" That will allow your brain to search for those reasons for why you originally fell in love, and this will help you to recall those memories.

Love and joy are one and the same! When you choose the energy of love, even when you are not feeling it, you act in a way that manifests more joy into your life. The wonderful thing about this is, no matter the outcome of your relationship, you will be elevating the energy of love around you and that will attract more love from every corner of your life. This can only positively impact your relationship. Even in the worst-case scenario, if your partner is not in the right energetic space to be uplifted by your energy, you will be able to move on from the relationship with ease and joy. When in doubt, always choose love!

Now, if you ask yourself the question, "Why is it so easy for me to choose love and compassion in all that I do?" you will find that your thinking begins to expand in all areas of your life. At first, it may seem like a tall order to try to do this in every moment of your life. But let us think for a moment about the alternative: If you respond from places of anger and frustration, hurt feelings and diminished self-esteem, then how would that make you feel? Sometimes people feel that it is a point of self-respect to express anger toward another person. But would this actually lead to feelings of joy? In most cases the answer will be no. You would create only more hurt feelings, hostility, and pain—which draws more of this energy to you and causes the cycle to be repeated!

As an example of breaking a painful cycle by choosing love, I want to share a reading that Gerry and I did not too long ago for a woman who was in the process of divorce. Sally (not her real name) was living with her mother, who had been a source of substantial pain while Sally was growing up. She was often compared to her sister, whom she was never able to measure up to. The mother was always hostile, emotionally unsupportive, and critical. Now this poor woman found herself having to live with her mother until the divorce was finalized and she could get back on her feet.

We spoke about how the mother-daughter relationship and resulting soul loss had caused Sally to attract the energy of her marriage. Now she was at a point where she wanted to take her power back, but she felt vulnerable in her childhood home. I told Sally that people who are critical are actually lacking energy; when they encounter someone vibrating at a higher level, they will try to put the person down in order to temporarily steal some of that energy. Nasty comments send energetic hooks through the other person's solar plexus chakra. However, this lift generally lasts a short time because self-esteem issues quickly dissolve it.

Since Sally needed to live there for a while and could not change her environment, I advised that she try to understand that her mom's criticism was not really about her. It was truly about how Sally's elevated energy was making her mom feel "less than" because her mom's energy was from a lower, sadder vibration. We talked about not feeding into the energy of the anger, but rather walking away and feeling compassion—and also asking for a legion of angels to surround the two of them. The next time that we spoke, Sally said her situation with her mother had substantially improved; she'd even found herself acting as her mom's defender when her mom had been "too nice" to someone else. The power of choosing love is truly amazing!

∽

While many of you may feel as though you have experienced someone trying to steal your energy, you might not realize that you have most likely been a "taker" as well. Consider an argument with another person in which the exchanges have been hurtful and you are feeling depleted; then you say something that wounds the other person and this give you a little energetic boost. This type of give-and-take happens in all relationships.

Sometimes depleted energy in relationships occurs through more subtle ways. It happens when you are young and you are always the last one picked for a sports team. It happens when you are not asked to dance. It happens when you are made fun of. It happens when you ask someone out and they reject you. It happens when your partner cheats on you. It happens when your best friend takes someone else's side in an argument. It happens when your work mate undermines you for a promotion. It happens when you get a divorce. It happens when you beat yourself up for not being "enough." Every day of your life, there is the possibility that someone will do something that puts you in the position of having to choose to act from a place of love and compassion or from a place of fear, anger, or even hatred. *Leslie Keith,* a Soul Coach® from Alberta, Canada, addresses this very quandary when she asks:

> *How can we know when enough is enough in work, relationships, or families? When have things gone against the grain long enough to break off a relationship—are these relationships ever really severed? Why does it seem like people who are unfeeling to others continue to have things their way?*

This question gives voice to the frustration that many feel when they are in a similar situation. The key to knowing how to deal with all of this goes back to being able to answer two questions: "What could I do in this situation that would bring me the most joy?" and "How can I find the positive energy and power that is hidden behind this challenge?"

It may be difficult to keep these questions in mind when you are growing up and friends are being mean to you in grade school; but if you are taught to think this way, it will lead to a happier life. When you are an adult, these questions become easier to look at honestly, and doing so will help you to make almost any relationship decision. For example, let us say that you are having a conflict with a family member, and you are invited to a wedding that they will be attending. You think to yourself: *What would bring me the most joy?* You start examining how important it is for you to go to the wedding and what emotions the event calls up for you. You consider whether it might cause more stress than joy, and whether you will be sad to miss it. You wonder if not going would be denying yourself the possibility to experience joy. Then you look to the second question: *How can I find the positive energy and power that is hidden behind this challenge?* Clearly, this could be an opportunity for you to resolve your differences with the other family member. Maybe that person is actually in your soul group and is giving you the opportunity to increase your vibration by helping you practice love, compassion, and forgiveness.

When you ask these two questions, it will always help you identify what is important to you and how you can grow from an experience. Remember that inside you and every human being there is divine life force. If you seek to connect with that energy, if you ask for your soul to speak to their soul to bring peace to your situation, you may be surprised at the results. Just remember that it is more important to be joyful than it is to be right!

However, when you are around someone who is unable to accept or process love, and it is actually damaging your ability to feel joy, then it is best to remove yourself from that energy. You can love and forgive someone from a distance. This is especially true when you are in a physically or emotionally abusive relationship.

I know that it may seem like selfish or self-obsessed people always get want they want. They are, after all, centering all of their thoughts and attention on the things they want—so it is no wonder that they are manifesting more of those things into their lives than a person who is always focused on doing things for others. And this is a perfect example of being able to learn from even very self-serving people. If you do focus on your own joy, then it is possible to create it! There is no reason that a self-serving person should be able to manifest joyful experiences while you cannot. You just have to believe that you deserve it as much as they believe that they do.

Since souls expand by experiencing the polarity of energy, then it seems clear that you would grow the most from relationships with the people who are most different from you. However, it is still true that like energy attracts like energy. So if there is someone in your life, then it is because they either possess a similar quality to you or they possess a quality that you would like to have. If you find yourself resenting the good-looking guy getting the attention of all the girls at the bar, then you desire to possess that charisma and attraction. Sometimes the people who have the things you lack are there to show you that you are just as deserving of joy!

For now, however, let us take a moment to remember that not every relationship is a challenge. There is love and support being sent to you from all around, even if that energy is not coming from the person that you are putting your energy into. Remember that whatever energy you create will come back to you. So if you love someone and they do not send you love in return, you will still receive loving energy through another person or experience. And if that love energy does come back to you from your romantic partner, please cherish and be grateful for it.

Always focus on what you love about your partner rather than on that which aggravates you. Imagine the difference in energy you would generate if you sat your partner down for a serious talk and proceeded to tell them all the things they did that made you feel loved. You would describe how much you appreciated all the tasks they do, from taking out the garbage to cooking dinner. Imagine how much they would then want to expand their loving actions— much more than if you started the conversation with all the things they did wrong and what they needed to change!

∽

One person who knows well the power of love and passion is **Meggan Watterson**, author of *How to Love Yourself (and Sometimes Other People)*. She is the founder of REVEAL, an organization that spiritually empowers women to connect to the love within them, reclaim their bodies as sacred, and become soul-led agents of change in the world. She was so very kind to offer her story of love and angelic influence, and I would like to offer it to you in her own words:

I have met my soul mate, or a soul mate. I deeply believe he is the love of my life. Last winter, we were brought together by a woman inviting me to the spiritual retreat center where they both work to teach a program based on my first book, Reveal. It was love at first sight for me. A deep, bone-knowing recognized him. I told him that first night, "I'm so grateful you exist." And now, a year later, that gratitude still radiates every time we are with each other.

I dreamed of meeting him about 12 years before we met; I was given the word devon in the dream. This past weekend we stayed at the inn at the end of his street, the Devonfield Inn. (Smile.) Our connection sometimes is so powerful and in a way so "beyond" us that we are moved to tears, rendered silent because there are no words in the depths of the soul.

The ego-me imagined that when I met with this "devon" man, he would know me, too. Of course, a smooth, natural unfolding would happen between us, and our relationship would deepen with ease. (Smile.) The reality is that we have both gone through intense ego-dismantling, a process that has been both painful and powerfully healing. I feel free in a way I never have before. I also feel radiantly alive.

We struggle sometimes with wondering if we can do this intense soul-work and also be life partners. Is there a way to have heaven here in the everyday? Can a love this epic also exist in daily doses? We go through states of union and then of separation—and we are intensely aware of them. This plays itself out as well because we physically live in separate states right now.

One evening that we were in one of our phases of physical separation, I was feeling so far from him—and I began to pray. I felt from the beginning that we are deeply supported by the spiritual realm. So instead of just suffering and wondering and longing, I asked the angel of our relationship to appear. I usually experience an encounter with angels from within me, in my heart. But this was very different. I felt the physical presence of someone enter my bedroom. I sat up in bed with a gasp. I couldn't see anyone but I knew that I wasn't alone. It kind of freaked me out; it was so immensely real. I sensed that this presence was to the right of the bed. I looked in that direction and for a brief moment saw a flash of the most vibrant red I have ever seen. I got chills *and my palms started to sweat. Then I heard a voice from within me say, "He's with you . . . Even now. Everything is as it should be. He loves you as you love him." Then I saw an image of the infinity symbol, and a tremendous wave of calm washed over me. A profound courage came to the surface of me, and I knew that everything would be okay. This doesn't mean that I knew what would happen in the course of our relationship, or if it would end in this lifetime. I just knew that whatever unfolds, I will become more love because of us!*

My question then for you, Margaret, is: How do we know if a soul mate can also make a loving life partner?

First I want to thank you, Meggan, for sharing such a personal story and asking such a powerful question! Many of you have found someone whom you believe in your heart is your soul mate. In this sense, I mean that this person has unlocked in you, and you in them, an experience akin to the level of love you feel as your higher self. It is a feeling that goes beyond the time and space of human existence. This person has come into your life to help take you to the highest expression of your soul within this body—and you do the same for them.

The answer to your question, Meggan, which I know you already know, is that you can't know whether someone, even your soul mate, will be your partner for life. The infinity symbol in your vision is a reference to the deep level of complexity and indestructibility in your relationship. It also speaks to the truth that all relationships (at a soul level) are infinite. So when one takes that type of energy and worries whether it will last through this incarnation, it is almost as though you are inadvertently sending out an energetic message that is limiting the belief in this love. When you project into the future and wonder if a love will be with you over the course of a lifetime, you are essentially attempting to place an unmeasurable feeling into a measurable amount of time.

I share the rest of this message for Meggan, but also for all of you reading this. In this physical incarnation you are experiencing, there are many from your soul group who have incarnated with you that could potentially be your soul mate. In this case, I do not use the term to signify a romantic relationship; this is a relationship you chose in your soul state, someone to come into your lifetime to help you grow and for you to help them to grow. Sometimes that growth will be light and easy, while at other times it will be more of a challenge. This is the ego-dismantling referred to in Meggan's story—learning that you need not be in control of all the variables in order to be happy in life. In fact the more that you try to control the relationships around you, the more you will find yourself being met with resentment and mixed emotions. The more you allow the situations in your life to flow freely, the easier your relationships will be because you stop creating expectations that will ultimately lead to disappointment. If you are a controlling person, more love will flow to you if you loosen the controls. If you find yourself in a relationship in which you are being controlled, ask your angels to help you to see what this person has to show you about yourself. What are *you* trying to control?

∽

I'd like to close this chapter with a story from Gerry's life, in which he gains a deeper understanding of himself and relationships. In his words:

> When I was learning to be a massage therapist, the instructor told the class that when we began to work on clients, we might notice our own physical pain being magnified, and our clients might talk about situations in their lives that would greatly mirror our own. She suggested that everyone be mindful of that and to work on our personal issues so as not to have the energy amplified!
>
> At this point, I had just gotten divorced for the second time. My first wife was going through an ever-growing depression and sometimes psychotic behavior (five years later she would take her own life), and I kept getting pulled into the spiraling chaos of her life in order to try to protect my children. She'd been causing ongoing damage to my second

marriage with constant threats and intense drama, until finally my exhausted second wife couldn't take the insanity and ended the relationship.

The one thing I was certain of was that something within me was attracting these problems to my relationships, so I started to attend Co-Dependents Anonymous (CoDA) meetings. This is a 12-step program modeled after Alcoholics Anonymous that focuses on helping people who do not have healthy, functioning relationships. I listened intently to the stories people shared at every meeting; I was so happy to hear that I was not alone in my thinking and my issues. Long before I knew about anything remotely metaphysical, I seemed to be feeling some relief by turning over my worries and concerns to this unknown "higher power." One night, after a CoDA meeting, I had a dream that recalled a real-life memory I had not thought about in years:

When I was about five years old, my parents took me to an amusement park a couple of towns away. This was around the time that helium-filled balloons started to be sold, and I excitedly asked my parents for one. They bought it for me, but my mom tied it to my wrist so that it wouldn't float away and turn into a waste of money. My parents had been struggling hard financially, so every expense was carefully budgeted for by my mom.

As we walked around the park and took in the sights, I heard a woman yelling. I turned around to see her scolding a little boy, about my age, who had just let go of his balloon. Despite the fact that she was quite upset, the little boy had a smile on his face as his eyes followed the balloon up into a night sky that was all lit up by the amusement park rides. At one point the little boy saw me looking at the balloon, too; our eyes met and we shared a smile. Then we both went back to looking at the balloon, mesmerized as it floated higher and higher, until it was out of sight. When it was gone we broke into laughter, and the other little boy continued to laugh as his mother dragged him away, still yelling about the lost money. On the ride home I kept looking at the sky, hoping for a glimpse of the balloon somewhere up there.

When I got home, my mom took the balloon from my wrist and tied it to the railing of my bed so that it couldn't fly out the open window. I went to sleep looking at my balloon hovering by my bed, thankful that I had not lost it like that other little boy—but smiling as the memory of the balloon's flight crossed my mind. Of course, the first thing I did when I awoke the next morning was look for my balloon floating above me—but it wasn't there. It had deflated, and the string now hung below my bed, the shriveled balloon on the floor. My mom and dad comforted my tears, saying that it must have been defective and my dad would talk to the man to get a new one the next time we went. (At the time, no one really knew about how helium leaked out of porous balloons.) I wished then that I had let my balloon fly like the other boy had. If I had known this was going to happen, I would have let go and let it fly free!

The feeling from the dream stayed with me when I awoke. Later that day, I had to pick up some things left at the house following my recent divorce, so I drove to where my ex-wife and I had lived. This is an area blessed with constant sightings of hot air balloons; it even hosted the state's annual balloon festival. I loved that festival and had always dreamed of taking a hot air balloon ride—until I discovered that pilots have no real control over the direction of a balloon other than taking it up and bringing it down. The rest of the trip was really up to the wind! After having lived through a marriage that was filled with chaos and unpredictability, I liked predictability; I liked knowing where I was taking off and where I was landing and I liked the security of knowing where I would be setting my feet down.

Suddenly I was struck with the realization that all I wanted was to be in control, yet I had somehow created a life that was totally out of control. Why wasn't my desire working? My thoughts went back to the dream of the night before, and I understood why. "Control" was when my mom tied the balloon to my wrist; I had the pleasure of it for a short time and then it was gone! But the other little boy experienced true joy as he watched that balloon fly into the night sky. It was then that I knew that all I ever really wanted was *freedom*. This wasn't a desire to not be in a relationship, but a fear that I was going to lose that person—and the energy of this fear had already cost me two relationships.

Dear ones, you are all probably familiar with the saying, "If you love something, set it free. If it comes back, it is yours. If it doesn't, it never was." The truth is that no other person, and no relationship, is ever truly yours! But the more freedom you give for a person to do what their soul desires, which is to expand its energy, then the more they will love and appreciate you—thus expanding your soul.

Let go of your balloons, dear ones!

CHAPTER
SEVEN

SEX AND
THE ART OF
NONJUDGMENT

> *"At a soul level, you have no judgment
> as to how you identify yourself sexually."*

One of the most confusing areas of understanding for humans is that of sexuality. Sex so often gets lumped together with shame due to certain societal and religious views. The original concept behind creating regulations in regard to sexuality was in the interest of the protection of property. Wives, children, and animals were considered extensions of a man's personal property, so societal laws were created to protect them. Echoes of this perspective can be seen in the modern mind-set, as society still considers certain groups as being *less than* the structures in power that are meant to "protect" them.

This makes author, sex educator, and artist **Barbara Carrellas** the perfect person to introduce our discussion. I would describe Barbara as a "sexual anthropologist," as she studies how societies view sex and always looks to expand positive energy throughout the world by influencing our attitudes toward this loving act. She is the author of *Ecstasy Is Necessary: A Practical Guide* and *Urban Tantra: Sacred Sex for the Twenty-First Century*. Barbara asks:

> *So many of our beliefs about sexual preferences, gender identity, and rules for healthy relationships have been based on binaries. You're either straight or gay, you're normal or a pervert, you're male or female, you're either monogamous or you're cheating. Now that's all changing. People are rejecting these either/or choices. There are people who identify as sexually fluid, gender queer, consciously kinky, and polyamorous (just to name a few of these binary busters). Why has this all exploded in just the past few years? Will it last?*

You are correct that it does "appear" that binary busters have exploded in just the past few years. In truth, however, there have been other periods of history where sexuality was much more "fluid," as you have so well stated it. Most of the changes that are happening now are not just about the energy of sexuality but rather about the soul desiring to express its true nature.

Many cultures see sexuality as a function of society rather than as a vehicle to seek your ultimate bliss. However, sexual energy is generated neither by the body nor by the mind—it is a creative energy that comes from the essence of the soul itself! It is the feeling of expanding energy and extreme bliss, which is difficult to contain in a human form. When your soul incarnates into a certain human form more frequently than another, then your energy might identify with aspects of the most frequently incarnated form. This influences the gender that you feel attracted to as well as the gender that you identify with—regardless of the gender that you are born into! From this, many self-identify with labels such as gay, lesbian, bisexual, transgender, etc.

At a soul level, you have no judgment as to how you identify yourself sexually, regardless of the human form that you have taken, or if you make the conscious decision to alter that human form. The only thing that is important to you as a soul is that you continue to seek opportunities to expand your energy and that you express joy in all of your experiences. So if at some point in your incarnation you decide that you are a man who is attracted to other men, that is not considered "wrong." The only issue is whether you allow yourself to express this energy in a loving and compassionate manner toward yourself and others or whether you hide and contain this energy because you are afraid of how the world will react to your decision.

Your higher selves see so many humans ultimately fearing to be themselves because of their family, societal, or religious situations. This fear-based reaction prevents their soul energy from growing because they are restricting the flow of love and compassion. Your souls desire to expand the universe through thought, yet find that they are facing a tumultuous battle in this area of sexuality: One day there is an expansion of acceptance; the next day a setback moves the energy toward fear. So they are encouraging human beings to experiment with new approaches in the best interest of expanding love, compassion, and joy; and this is what is causing the binary busters you have noticed.

For example, at a basic level, what has expanded the gay rights movement has been more than the political battles that have been waged. Instead, love and compassion have become part of the collective thought form. Individual thoughts build momentum as they are shared by the higher selves to become a collective thought form, which becomes a framework to turn the thoughts into a joint consciousness on the physical plane. When many people realized that they had a loved one who identified with a different sexuality than the norm, they found themselves in the quandary of having to decide who was wrong—and they chose love. They responded with compassion. They decided that no one is wrong, you are entitled to your thinking and they are entitled to their thinking. And that, dear ones, is the posture of the soul. No one is right, no one is wrong, there is only the overwhelming desire to express the bliss of the soul through our bodies, and whatever feels right is fine!

This touches upon the other identifiers: "polyamorous" or even "consciously kinky." I think the latter is my favorite new phrase because it speaks to something interesting. If you accept that your human form is being "life-supported" by some energy outside of itself, and you call that energy your consciousness, then to be "consciously kinky" means that you are seeking to explore your sexuality in a way that feels comfortable to you—because it is tapping into your consciousness! *Kinky* essentially refers to an expression of sexuality that "bends" what is traditionally accepted. But unlike a kink in a hose that keeps what you desire from flowing, a kink in a sexual relationship can often expand the playfulness and joy of the expression, which allows the energy to flow more freely!

Conscious kink is not something that is experienced just by small groups of individuals in a society. For example, *50 Shades of Grey,* one of the most popular books of the last couple of years—which became one of the most anticipated movies—revolved around the story of a young woman who found herself attracted to a very successful man who expressed his sexuality through sadomasochism. Although there has been criticism of certain aspects of the story, I believe that what many people are responding to is the way this woman decided to surrender herself to this man as well as how he, in many ways, learned how to surrender himself to his feelings for her.

Trust and surrender are important parts of exploring different forms of sexual pleasure, just as opening your mind and appetite expands the potential pleasures when trying new types of food. You may think that something is not to your taste until you try it—and then find that it becomes one of your favorite foods. The same can be said for different forms of sexual expression. Whether it is food or sex, most humans will try something different if they feel a sense of trust for the other person who is giving them the opportunity to explore it. You may find you like it or you may find it is not to your taste, but trust and surrender are the common threads of what allows you to try anything new.

Remember that the chakra responsible for generating all of your creative energy is the same one that generates your sexual energy. So it should not come as any great surprise that you might find this chakra opening you up to being "creative" when it would come to experiencing sexual bliss.

As the souls of human beings evolve—and make no mistake, despite what you might consider the hopelessness of the human condition at times, you *are* evolving—it is causing you to move toward seeking more joy in your personal experiences. The soul is well aware that this requires a life that is filled with love, compassion, and a lack of judgment for others. Many of those who are expanding their ability to love without judgment are also finding that this is expanding their ability to love more than one human being with the same intensity. This then gives birth to what is called the polyamorous movement. Again, at a soul level, if you are expressing love and joy and you are sharing that experience with like-minded individuals—without the desire to hurt, harm, or control another person in any way—then there is no judgment in this regard. It is likely that as more expansive, open thought continues to develop, more "open relationships" will as well. Perhaps it is also this need for the soul to seek growth through new experiences that lies at the root of the high divorce rates that many countries are experiencing.

Thought is constantly expanding and, as it does, so will the confines of sexuality. What stands to be determined is how quickly society will grow along with it!

∞

I have often used the analogy of life being a movie with all of you as the leads of your amazing stories. Your role as a "performer" is probably never stronger than it is when you are involved in a sexual relationship. Sex is the only "skill" on the planet that everyone is supposed to be expert in—without having received any training and while being at their most exposed and vulnerable at the same time! The concept of being a virgin has actually begun to have a stigma attached to it; rather than celebrating innocence and the exciting new world that lies ahead, many virgins feel they must make up for their lack of experience somehow. New lovers expect their first time together to be magical, regardless of the fact they have had no time to get to know the other's preferences or sensitivities. We do not understand why you have done this to yourselves, embracing this narrative of performance rather than honest communication. Your inability to talk to each other about sex so that you can learn more stems from the element of shame. Most young people find it gross to imagine their parents having sex, while most parents don't want to think about their little one having sex. The result is that neither wants to speak to the other about the topic. As you continue to evolve, I am sure that you will develop better ways of communication, and you will enjoy the beautiful process of sex without feeling like it must be a performance!

One very literal demonstration of sex as a performance, which is also a way that many people learn about sex, is pornography. While there are great debates about this type of filmmaking, I must say that at a soul level it is seen as just another type of storytelling. What changes it from a fun, distracting, and sometimes informative form of entertainment to a dangerous obsession is not the result of the making of the film but the result of the psychological state of the viewer.

Many adult performers see themselves as creating products that can actually help lead toward a healthier, more open, and playful attitude about sex. And many of them, like many of you, are deeply spiritual people. Such is the case for adult-film star *Bailey Jay*. She is a tireless advocate for the rights of transgender people, and while she is serious about equality she also has a wonderful sense of humor that allows her to be self-effacing and lighthearted about most everything in life. Gerry and Bailey met as a result of Bailey looking to help people, especially many transgender people, to heal their sexual guilt. One of her dreams is to develop a spiritual healing center near her home in the state of New York, and her question speaks to how you can tie in the sexual world with the rest of your world.

Bailey asks:

Do you believe sex could be incorporated into a spiritual/healing practice, or should they be kept separate?

I love how this question reflects the desire to blend the worlds of body and spirit, but the truth is that they are *already* blended. Sexual energy is spiritual, or soul, energy. So when you are feeling it, you are experiencing a spiritual energy, especially when it is allowed to be felt in a playful, joy-filled way. The physical process is also extremely healing because it produces chemicals in the brain that reduce stress and induce a sense of well-being.

Sexual energy, which is essentially one of the most profound expressions of joy that humans experience, is created at the level of the higher self. This filters down to the physical level, so when you are attracted to another person, it creates a response within your body that elevates your personal desire to create an experience of sexual pleasure. It is often very difficult for humans to wrap their minds around the concept of how to create self-joy in their daily lives, and to accept the importance of focusing their time, attention, and emotions directly on themselves. But most humans *will* allow themselves self-gratification when their body creates the energy and desire for sexual pleasure. Masturbation is an act of self-love, and very often it is accompanied by vivid fantasies, even for people who are not usually able to create clear pictures about other things. That is because your sexual energy is created in the same chakra that produces your creative energy. And that creative energy of fantasy, coupled with the physical action of honoring the body's desire to feel pleasure and be touched, results in the manifestation of the full-body sensation that you refer to as *orgasm*. I use the word *manifestation* because sexual energy is one of the purest forms of manifesting energy that you possess—and without the judgment and the guilt about self-love, you would be able to harness so much more power in this area.

Sexual fantasy is one area in which you allow yourself to have whatever experience you would like to have, with whomever you would like. What makes this such a powerful experience of manifestation is that you are imagining a potential occurrence as though it were happening right now, and then, through the act of self-love, allowing yourself to feel the pleasure of what that experience would feel like *in the present moment.* So you are doing all of the most essential things that would allow manifestation to occur in your regular thinking but with one major difference: you have become so accustomed to the understanding that this experience is *not* real that, as soon as it is over, you negate the reality of the fantasy you just created, sometimes going a step further and feeling guilty for having imagined it.

Men have made many laws and customs that regard masturbation as a shameful act. This is because one of the ways that people in power maintain their status is by ensuring that others do not feel powerful. Certain cultures consider masturbation especially bad when done by women, as they do not want women to feel any possibility of power or sexual pleasure without a man. Regardless, the act has continued to thrive throughout human evolution and is now becoming more accepted because more people are rebelling against the control of thought! Your unencumbered thoughts during your sexual fantasies are your personal manifestations—and this is the one place that people can feel free! Because there is a release of brain chemicals at the time of orgasm that makes this free thought feel pleasurable, people continue to do it, and what is so positive about this is that it demonstrates a clear connection to your soul essence and the soul's desire to experience freedom and joy.

As I have already mentioned, you as a soul have no problem with sex, fantasies, or masturbation. We as angels have no judgment about it either, nor does the Creator. They are merely a part of your creative expression and desire to experience joy. The only time this would be problematic is if it were to infringe on someone else's freedom and you force, coerce, or manipulate someone into fulfilling your fantasy—especially when that person might be too young, infirmed, or vulnerable to be within their power to consent.

I would like to suggest what may be taken as a very controversial idea, one that actually brings together the worlds of sexuality, spirituality, and healing, as Bailey was suggesting. Imagine that you are having a conflict with your partner, and you usually release stress through a fantasy about being with someone else. If you instead fantasize about being with your partner and sharing amazing love and bliss, the release that you feel becomes a very healing energy, because it relaxes your anger and aids in producing those same feelings you fantasized about. When you were in the early days of a relationship, your fantasies were about that very person you are currently with—so remembering each other and seeing each other from those early days while creating a wonderful orgasmic energy actually helps create a loving energy around the relationship.

Now imagine for a moment that while you were allowing yourself the act of self-love, you were not thinking about sex at all. What if you were to think about other pleasurable things that you would like to manifest into your life? Suppose you were thinking about how amazing it would feel to do the work you would like to perform for the money you would like to make. You have become conditioned to think that when you perform the physical act of self-love, your thoughts should only be about sex. But self-love is about *self-love,* so begin to expand your thinking in this area by allowing yourself to think about other things that would bring you joy. When you actually *feel* the sensation of pleasure in the present moment in connection to those thoughts, you create a very strong emotional and physical response and make your manifestation much stronger. While you may not think that this is occurring, please realize that you are working with powerful energy that is coming from your creative center. In addition, you are removing the feeling of shame that so many feel around the act of physical self-love. This is helpful, as your brain internalizes that guilt and translates it into the thought form "I feel guilty when I have pleasurable thoughts and when I love myself."

In the same way, if you are completely present when you are with your sexual partner, you can share a powerful energy between you two by having a playful talk about all the places you can make love when you manifest your great fortune or travel all over the world. Together, you can make your pleasurable act in the present moment a method of manifesting more pleasure in the future.

So yes, dear ones, it is possible for you to consciously pull the manifesting capacity of your soul and the sensation capacity of your body into unison to create orgasmic possibilities!

∽

Finally, on the connection between the world of spirit and the physical, I wanted to respond to a question that was posed by *Linda Crea,* a spiritual energy healer from Southington, Connecticut. Linda asks:

It seems that spirits are not afraid to share, so how much of our sex life is seen? I have been told that souls have filters, but is that the truth?

Your higher self is aware of your actions, dear one, but the information that is uploaded to the collective souls is about the energy that is created by physical experiences. This forms the filter that you are speaking about. It is certainly of interest to a soul to know how physical creatures harness the energetic power of sexual energy, but they are receiving that information as you are uploading it to them rather than hovering above your bedroom actually watching. There is also a great respect for you, so no guide or spirit will visit your physical world without permission, unless you are in some type of danger and you have previously asked them to aid in your protection. I hope that this helps to answer your question, and I thank you for it because there are many others around the world who wonder the same thing!

A PURR-FECT WORLD

The Healing Power of Animals

> *"The same soul energy that inhabits humans*
> *also inhabits the forms of all the*
> *creatures on your planet."*

In the amazing physical structure that is your planet Earth, there were created thousands of species who help to hold together the balance of your world. They all, in some way, impact you and the preservation of the planet, but some have a more personal influence. You have come to call these creatures *pets.* The physical act of petting that you are drawn to do in their presence brings pleasure to both of you, and there is tremendous love that is shared in the process even when you are not concentrating on it. These companions create bonds with humans that seem to defy explanation, as wellness activist and *New York Times* best-selling author, **Kris Carr,** can attest. With deep emotion Kris writes:

My precious cat Crystal was like a daughter to me. She passed away a few years ago, and I miss her terribly. Recently, my sweet hound Buddy was diagnosed with the canine version of ALS (Lou Gehrig's Disease). It's so hard losing our fur children, just writing this question makes me tear up. I don't know how long Buddy has left with us and I'm wondering a few things. Will he tell me when it's time for him to go? Can I talk to him when he's gone, will he still be with me? I already believe that animals have souls, like us, I'm just not sure how to connect and feel their presence. Because I can't have children of my own, my pets are my family and I hope to strengthen our bond in life and beyond.

My dearest Kris, it is so wonderful to have the opportunity to answer your very profound and heartfelt question. You spoke to a belief in animals having souls, which is not only true, but in fact animals have the very *same* souls that also inhabit human forms. At this very point in time, Kris, your higher self has taken part of its energy and placed it all over the planet in 4 distinct human forms as well as in over 150 different animal forms! While this might come as a bit of a shock to you, on the other hand it may help you to make some sense of why you feel such a sense of affinity to various creatures. You can actually sense that there is a soul essence to them that is of an equal importance to yours!

In many ancient and indigenous cultures there was an acknowledgment of the sacredness of all life forms. Everything was viewed as having a spirit, a soul. There was a deep reverence and respect for all creatures, because they knew that all of life had a purpose. Even if the purpose was to act as food for the tribe, they would ask for the spirit of that animal to live on within them, so that they could better know and honor it for sharing its life. You are deeply in touch with this sense—so much so that part of your essence is to not ingest food that came from another being.

Domestic animals have been a part of the culture of mankind for centuries. Cats were revered in ancient Egypt, and dogs have been companions and helpers for thousands of years. Humans have felt a very special connection to these two species in particular because they are, in many ways, the closest to you in energetic consciousness—and also because they offer important examples of what is actually necessary to profoundly enjoy your human experience.

It has often been said that dogs are so popular because they offer unconditional love and complete loyalty to their owners. They are deeply sensitive, protective, and loyal; but they also evoke love in just as powerful a manner as they offer it, having perfected the ability to celebrate every moment of life! They celebrate waking, walking, playing, eating, pooping; there is not an aspect to their day that they do without joy. This is because they can feel your heavier energy, and they want to help you to "lighten the load," so to speak, so that you can be happy like them. That is also why they can sense when you are sick, troubled, or sad.

There is an erroneous concept that dogs have very poor short-term memory because they will respond to their human returning home in the same manner whether they have been gone for five minutes or five hours. As humans, you assume that this is a design defect! But dogs are simply capable of allowing their hearts to feel unfettered emotion, which is what makes them so very appealing to humans. There are very few human relationships that do not have some sort of expectations and conditions connected to the release of love, emotion, and playfulness. So, in many ways, that which you cannot perfect in your human existence, you do perfect when you incarnate as a dog.

Cats offer humans a different lesson in understanding themselves: a strong role model of self-actualization and self-care, while still offering love, acceptance, and playfulness. Cats do not seek to first please you; they are more independent. They seek to first take care of their immediate needs, and only then will they expand this care to others. Cats are sublimely happy to find a sunny spot to nap in and feel no guilt in doing so. Despite the schedule of the family, cats will make their own hours. They will eat only when they are hungry, drink when they are thirsty, and seek companionship when they are comfortable to do so. When they do seek companionship, they are so intense in the release of their loving energy that it creates the distinct vibration known as a purr. Think of the purr as *pure,* the clear and unencumbered essence of the energy being created by the cat. When it purrs, it has moved into an elevated state that causes it to literally vibrate at a much higher level! This vibration is not only felt by the cat—who is essentially experiencing a state of bliss—but also those around it. This is why humans find it so pleasant to hold or pet a purring cat. The energy is both relaxing and healing, and it enters the bodies of those in contact.

You know in your heart, Kris, that all of this is true because this is the essence that you felt with your cat, Crystal. I love that you refer to her as your "daughter," as her soul essence has been family with you on many other occasions, and she did so much to offer you healing energy to help with your own recovery. It is healthier to consider your pet companions as children, a being entrusted to your care, than as creatures that you "own." In truth, you own nothing on this planet; this is an illusion that mankind has created to meet their desire for a sense of permanence and abundance. But when you "parent" another being, that is a completely different thing! The word actually comes from a Latin word meaning to "bring forth." So in parenting your animal companions, you are fulfilling one of the purposes of the soul, which is to uplift other souls and expand love and compassion. In particular, when you rescue animals, you seek to uplift their spirits to a new place of joy and allow them to be the essence of who they are, and they in turn uplift your soul and help you reach new heights of love and compassion!

This brings me then to your question of communication between souls and, more specifically, your son, Buddy. He loves you with all his heart and soul, and his higher self has been one of your closest soul friends. For Buddy, the hardest thing about leaving will be the pain that it will cause you, as dogs are so empathetic to pain and sadness and their greatest desire is to spread joy and love. It is very likely that as Buddy gets closer to transition, he will try to seek out a place away from you so he can be alone in his discomfort. When you begin to see him looking for places to hide and sense his body giving up, then it is time for his transition.

Some wonder whether it is proper to euthanize an animal. There are those who say it is playing God and not allowing nature to take its course, while others say it is inhumane to allow your children to suffer through an incurable illness. In your soul state, there is no judgment in this area. Your consciousness and your heart will move you to make the right decision for yourself. Remember that your soul seeks to expand love and compassion, so as long as these are the motivating actions, then your actions are consistent with your soul's desire.

Do not focus on your loved one's death but rather on their life. Every day, let Buddy know how much he means to you and call to mind at least one great memory you share while you cuddle and pet him. He needs to feel your joy about his life and not your pain and sadness in his illness or death. If you are going to be with him at the time of his passing, let him know that you will find joy every day in memories of what he has given to you and taught you. Let him know that you will miss him, but you are counting on him to use those hound skills to track you down and keep coming to you—and, trust me, he will do so! He needs to remember how much more powerful he is as pure energy than as a physical form.

But for now, allow for simple tasks so that Buddy still feels his importance to the family and the opportunities for "who's my good boy" abounding. Each night, get down on the floor with him, hold him, and allow yourself to go into a meditative state. As you breathe, visualize your breath and your energy merging with his. Remember that one of the original meanings of the word *animal* is "one whose life comes from breathing the air." As you connect with your higher self, imagine it then connecting with Buddy's. The reason that it is sometimes hard to connect with the energy of your dog or cat when you are in your regular state is that they actually vibrate at a higher frequency—so you have to elevate to theirs to communicate. Listening to drumming in the background may help; as you have done work as a shaman in the past, the drumming will reawaken how you communicate!

Remembering this essence of your shamanic self will help you to do just as you would like, which is to strengthen your bond in this lifetime and beyond!

∞

The topic of what happens to your pets when they cross over comes up so frequently, and I am so thankful for all your questions.

I share a few here that I think will help answer the most often asked. *Danielle Lewis,* a registered nurse from Cincinatti, Ohio, asks:

We have incredible bonds with our pets, and we miss them so when they pass. Are they available to connect with in heaven? Do they have angels to help them to pass?

The same soul energy that inhabits humans also inhabits the forms of all the creatures on your planet. As such, all animals are guided, protected, and assisted by the same angels, and those angels are there when they transition.

What is important to know is that once energy is created and put into the form of a physical being on this planet, whether that energy is in an animal or a human, it is recorded within the memory of the higher self. This distinct energy is essentially preserved for all time within the higher self. You are able to reconnect with and experience that energy again, either when you return to your soul state or now, if you call upon that energy for any reason.

∽

In regard to the reincarnation of your pets, *Alejandra Kate,* an empathetic medium and children's book author from Crestline, California, asks:

Do our animals incarnate back into each of our lives? For example, would my horse in a prior life come back as my parrot in this life? Or do animals always incarnate as the same species? Is it always a "once a cat always a cat" kind of thing?

Souls, dear Alex, incarnate in all forms of life: animal, plant, mineral, all types of elements, and, of course, human. There is no telling what life form a soul might choose from one incarnation to another. While you might like a particular form and could choose to come back in that form for multiple incarnations, you are certainly not bound to do so!

You tend to travel in soul groups, and levels of energetic affection grow between these souls, so you will sometimes encounter an animal that brings up a sense of affection in you similar to what you felt for another animal. You might think it is the same soul, and sometimes it is. Sometimes you will even encounter your own soul energy in an animal that comes into your life. This is a very interesting experience and happens quite frequently!

∽

Some of you have found yourself troubled by the circumstances faced by souls who incarnate as animals. *Indya Roberts,* a mum of two cats and a volunteer at an animal charity in Strasbourg, France, asks a question that so many of you who love animals think upon every day:

Why do so many millions of animals have to suffer such horrendous conditions? Will this ever end and can we do anything about it in the meantime? I am aware of a few purposes, one being to teach us unconditional love, but I was wondering if Margaret's angelic knowledge could help us understand exactly what is happening and how we can change things for the better so we could act in love and peace together and give our animal kingdom the happy, cruelty-free life they deserve. Animal lovers are really longing for the day when humans and animals would be equals living in harmony side by side.

Living in harmony is the goal for all souls on the planet. But what keeps humans from doing so is the illusion of separation that you have created within your human form. You see yourselves as being different from other humans, and see your uniqueness not as the thing that gives each of you the individual power and gifts that you bring to the world but rather as something that makes others different and not to be trusted. This actually makes humans feel very disempowered rather than empowered.

It is this sense of being disempowered that makes humans seek to have something that they can have power or dominion over. You seek something that you can clearly see as "less than" you. Some of you see this as meaning that they are more vulnerable life forms, and it causes you to be protective and want to care for them; others see these forms as something that can be manipulated and abused. The people who look at animals in the latter manner do not feel that way uniquely toward animals. Their sense of being powerless comes out in their interactions with humans as well, and they tend to be controlling and abusive in many areas of their lives. But it is far easier to be cruel when the object of your abuse is not able to fight back or voice complaint. Furthermore, many animals, especially dogs, will continue to love the abuser.

Animals are far more forgiving than humans because animals' vibration of love and compassion is so much higher. This love holds true even in the field of animal testing. The human life and condition is thought to be of more importance than that of an animal, so animals are used to test products, medicines, and such. If those doing the testing were to realize that their own soul might possibly be in the creature that they are testing on, then the desire to do so would be far different.

It is encouraging that you are evolving more and more each day in your awareness that all of life is sacred. Years ago, there was no such thing as animal activists. There were no groups that cared whether a company spilled oil that destroyed an ecosystem. Those who wished to communicate with animals were considered crazy, but now that is one of the fastest-growing movements of people to desire a personal *psychic* experience in a *mainstream* marketplace. So have hope, dear ones. If you are among those who have love for the other creatures of this world, please pray for legions of angels to protect them and your delicate ecosystem. And if you are among those who did not see how sacred all of life is, then know that we love you and that love extends to you from all the animal forms that you now are or will ever inhabit!

∼

I would like to close this chapter with a wonderful question sent in from *Niki Zamora,* a forensic scientist from San Diego, California, that looks at the much deeper question of what the energy of our animals can teach us on a soul level. She asks:

They say that when our friends (or loved ones) pass, they can become our spirit guides and help us from the other side. What I want to know is, what about pets that we have really loved and bonded with, when they pass can they also become our spirit guides and help us from the other side?

Your pets are souls that you live alongside as your higher self, so they are definitely with you and can assist you when they return to the state of their higher self. The energy that they possessed as your pet remains with them, and you may at times feel or sense that energy as its distinct vibration. (Every physical incarnation returns to soul state with its own energetic marking, which you refer to as DNA.) So you can ask to feel that distinct vibration or expression of their soul to assist you!

But I would just like to take this answer one step further in terms of expanding your knowledge as to how animal energy can help you from the soul level. You have probably all heard of the term *power animal*. It refers to a spirit guide in the form of an animal that assists you at various stages of your life when you are in need of a characteristic that is part of the essential power of that animal. Sometimes a soul might encounter one of its most powerful incarnations, not as a human but as an animal, and chooses to communicate from this form while retaining all of the knowledge it has gathered from its other incarnations. This soul makes the decision to expand the universe not by continuing to incarnate but rather by assisting other souls that are incarnated. They will offer the wisdom and powers that they have gathered from their incarnations to share with their mortal "students."

So when shamans reach out to the spirit world, they encounter these animals that come to offer guidance from the vantage point of their most powerful animal incarnation. The power animal that comes to assist you is very often the one that can bring you the strength that you most need to accomplish the task you are trying to accomplish. For example, when Gerry does soul retrieval, he has always encountered and been assisted by a striped tiger by the name of Metume. Tiger energy (medicine) is known to offer humans courage, focus, and the ability to seek and see visions; the tiger holds dominion over all. It also is capable of ferocious protection and kitten-like playfulness. During the soul-retrieval journeys, Metume provides guidance through any terrain, is always fearless and focused on recovering lost pieces, and communicates telepathically with great love. He is also capable of playfulness with younger returning soul pieces, which makes them feel an instant trust and rapport with him. He has been with Gerry through hundreds upon hundreds of journeys, and as a powerful soul guide he offers his amazing strengths to Gerry and others.

Other animal energies offer themselves to you at all times. You just need to be aware of them when they are happening. When you notice a butterfly hovering above you, it may have come to share an energy that you have been longing for. When a stray cat comes to your door or your house suddenly has spiders or bees, this might seem like an annoyance—but it also might be sending you some power that you have requested.

At one point during the writing of this book Gerry found that something always seemed to be distracting him, and he was growing frustrated with himself for these distractions. As he was sitting and trying to get a feeling for why this was happening, a small white spider lowered itself from the ceiling and hovered about three feet from his head. Gerry marveled that he could not see the invisible thread that the spider was hanging from, when the spider suddenly started to advance toward his head. Gerry's immediate reaction was to put up his hand—but then he recalled that perhaps this spider had come as a helper, and an interesting experience took place.

As Gerry moved his hand to the side, he could "see" that somehow the spider had sent a thread that was now attached to the palm of his left hand. As he moved his hand, the spider would move as well. The spider slowly began advancing on the thread, toward his palm, then stopped about one foot away. Suddenly Gerry felt his palm becoming very warm, and he could clearly feel that this spider had come to help him with something. The warmth continued for about three minutes, and then the spider advanced farther toward his palm, finally touching it and resting there for just a moment. It then retreated backward and began to throw threads that allowed it to move quickly away and upward, finally vanishing into the ceiling by a wood beam. As the sunlight came in through the window, for the first time Gerry was actually able to physically see the threads.

After the experience, he looked in his shamanic-medicine card book to see the power and medicine that the spider provided. The legend is that, within its web, spider created the first alphabet. Spiders have always been helping humans weave their stories and expand the ability to allow the "dream" world, the world of spirit, to be manifest in the physical world.

Following this experience, Gerry began to have visions of clarity about the book. He was able to reorganize the words I had already given him and feverishly write new words that I was sharing. Spider shared some powerful medicine, and your power animals will do the same for you if you are open to allowing their messengers to bring them to you.

Animals are your soul friends—incarnate and in spirit. Love them, cherish them, and preserve them, as they are doing the same for you!

DEATH, DYING, AFTERLIFE, REINCARNATION, AND KARMA

"So your higher self does retain the essence of emotions . . . Its actions are not driven by emotions but rather advised by them."

I am hopeful that by this point, we have clearly established that you are so very much more than you might have ever imagined. You are an eternal soul who places your energy in other life forms to expand your energy and the energy of the universe. Your higher self always exists and is constantly present, throughout all of your incarnations and throughout all of time. Here in this chapter, I wanted to be able to answer some of the more specific questions that so many of you posed about what happens when you leave this physical form. I would love to begin with a wonderful question that was brought to me by renowned meditation teacher and author of *Secrets of Meditation* and *destressifying*, **davidji.** He asks:

Are those who have left us to join the spirit realm capable of emotions as they watch over us, such as anger, disappointment, sadness, and joy? Or are they so merged with the divine flow of the universe that they are beyond emotions and only see us through a lens of unconditional acceptance and love?

When you are in your pure soul nature, which is the true eternal you that lends energy to your incarnations, you are a being of unconditional acceptance and love. The emotions that you feel as human beings are carried forward with you, however, so that they can be processed by your higher self and understood and shared with the collective souls of all that exists.

You upload information to your higher self all the time, which is then shared with the collective souls. But when the soul energy of your incarnation rejoins with your higher self, all of the emotions and conceptual energy of your experiences are retained, processed, and then merged into your higher self. In this fashion, the intellect can better understand the emotion and the emotion can better understand the intellect; and all that is processed through the lens of unconditional acceptance and re-created as loving knowledge and expansive energy.

So your higher self does retain the essence of emotions, but from an "overview," if you will. Its actions are not driven by emotions but rather advised by them. Those who have rejoined the spirit realm understand the emotions they have felt as humans, but they do not feel emotion in their current state other than that of love and acceptance.

~

Many humans who have lost loved ones suffer from the feeling of "unfinished business," believing that the one who has passed over still feels anger, hurt, or other negative emotion toward them. However, when a soul crosses over, there is nothing but unconditional love and total understanding that they feel toward those that they have left behind. You have likely heard stories of those who cross over, passing through a tunnel as they are drawn toward "the light." This tunnel is actually an energetic vortex that captures the vibration of emotional energy, memory, and any illness that has touched upon the spiritual DNA of the individual soul. Meanwhile the soul energy is cleansed as it moves toward reconnection with the higher self.

Of course, there are many who will not believe the words written in this book as a means to bring them peace. There are those who are uncertain of the existence of an afterlife. Sometimes your conscious beliefs are filled with doubt because your deeper, unconscious beliefs—your soul-based knowledge—are at odds with some of the popular terms or concepts relative to death. For example, if your soul's connection to your higher self is strong, but you are basically a logical person, it would be hard for you to believe in an "afterlife" because you sense that there is an "always life." In the same vein, you would find it hard to listen to terms like "perpetual rest" and "grant mercy on their soul" because you instinctively know that none of this rings true to you.

So for people who might be a bit more logical minded, there are earthly techniques to help with unresolved energy they feel toward loved ones, whether they are living or dead. One of these techniques is taught by psychic medium **Karen Noé**, author of *Your Life After Their Death*. She instructs people in the art of crafting letters to loved ones, either on this planet or in spirit. She essentially instructs the letter writer to *see through the other person's eyes* in terms of why someone did or didn't do certain things. There are different types of letters, including those asking forgiveness from someone you hurt, forgiving those who hurt you, telling others that you love them and why you are proud of them, and letters to oneself. Karen asks:

> *For years, and by angelic instruction, I have used the writing of letters to help people mend bridges with their loved ones who have gone back to spirit. I have also expanded this work for people to do with the living, so they can resolve the walls between them and lead happier lives. I have seen it change people's lives in both scenarios and wondered what is happening energetically in these letters that is causing this profound healing?*

Letter writing has always been a wonderful form of communication between humans for many different reasons. The written word has been used to note important moments in the history or culture of a people, to keep records of information, and to share stories. If you think back to the origins of the process, putting your thoughts and feelings down on paper was a way of recording them in physical form, as the spoken word was not held to as high a standard since it could be forgotten or misremembered. Even in the striking of agreements, when something could not be written down, people would seal their agreement with a handshake as an action that signified the word made physical.

In the days before other forms of communication were created, letter writing was a way for people to stay in contact over long distances. It was also sometimes a way for them to feel secure in saying deeply personal things that they may not be able to say in person. Even the modern tools of e-mail and texting are based in this tradition. There is something very important that happens when a thought is written down. The thought becomes a word and the word becomes recorded in a physical manifestation of the thought. It is therefore transformed and manifested into the physical realm.

In the work that you are doing, Karen, you are inviting others to partake in a process where distances are bridged, true emotions are allowed to be expressed, and thought is allowed to manifest. And the reason why this is so powerful is because the letters are a monologue that allows you to see the world through what you perceive to be the other person's eyes.

The beauty of the monologue is that it gives you the chance to say what it is that you want to say without fear of interruption by another person. Because you are writing it in a letter form, you are not just blurting it out but giving thought to what words should be put down. Since you are trying to write from the other person's viewpoint, you are giving power to the concept that there may be another point of view other than yours. That in itself lets you look into the situation from the perspective of your higher self, which then allows you to look into the other person's higher self. The result is a complete experience known as *insight*.

Insight, dear ones, is what you are always seeking to achieve as a soul. So when you take this opportunity to participate in this particular exercise, it is very powerful!

The concepts of death, the higher self, and reincarnation can get very complicated and become even more so when you begin to talk about communication with those who have passed on. *Leonarda Scandurra*, an administrative officer from Sydney, Australia, beautifully explains her conundrum:

There is one burning question I have always had that has not been answered for me. I believe our souls reincarnate into other forms when they are ready to. If this is the case, how do mediums connect with loved ones from the spirit world? For example, my father passed two years ago, and if he has incarnated again as another form, can a medium still connect to the spirit of my father? Or is he now not contactable as his soul has moved on to another form and may be living another life on Earth or another planet or realm?

When a medium reaches out to a soul who has returned to its essence, the medium is sensing and tuning into a vibration that is seeking to reach the person who has crossed over. That vibration is often assisted by a name or a birth date that helps the medium to tune in even more closely. Just try to picture tuning into a station on a radio dial. That tuning in allows them to reach that soul's frequency, which has since been merged into their higher self—their complete soul. The higher self will recognize the portion of itself that you are trying to reach and can then communicate back in the frequency of that person.

So you are reaching the higher self of your loved one, which can speak to you from the vibration of your loved one. That part of the higher self is exactly who you were looking to reach and has full memory of their physical past while continuing to feel deep love and affection for those left behind; but now it also has the depth of the combined knowledge of the higher self and other souls. This is why they seem to retain an essence of who they were, yet deeper and more profound, while still retaining all of the things that are associated with joy, like their sense of humor.

In the case of connection in a group setting, as you might see with mediums such as John Holland, the reverse actually happens. The soul that has passed, knowing that the people they left behind are in pain, helps guide those loved ones to someone who can reassure them that they are fine. They then create a hologram-like energy near the person they want to speak to, and the medium then taps into that energy form.

Even if the higher self puts part of its energy into another life form, you are still able to contact any life form that has crossed over. So reincarnation poses no problem. The higher self is monitoring thousands of incarnations at the same time, yet can very easily tap into the energy vibration and unique experiences of any component part of itself that has returned as well. Your father's incarnation was a part of the work of his higher self, and his higher self retains that memory. It is capable of now investing that energy in a new soul experience while still being able to access those experiences at any time. That is why you always hear me say that you have no idea how truly grand and amazing your higher self is and why we love and admire you so very much.

❧

I know that no matter how much you understand a concept from a spiritual and intellectual viewpoint, you are also a human being of flesh and blood, with very real emotions. So with great emotion comes this question from *Stephanie Tran,* of Guelph, Ontario, who lovingly describes herself as a full-time mom to an adorable daughter. She asks:

What can I do, or how should I proceed with my life, after a loved one has passed away suddenly and my heart is aching?

I can feel the pain in your question, dear one, and it is a pain that is all too familiar for many of you who are reading this. Death is very hard to cope with because you become so used to the presence of that person, and their filling your life with love. Or sometimes you lose someone that you did not have a close relationship with, and you now are aware that you will miss the opportunity to have that relationship. In either case, the sudden nature of death very often can cause soul loss, a deep loss of personal power. There are a few techniques that you can use to help move you forward from grief to the joy of the realization that your loved one now has the ability to be around you more than ever before. The following is what I would suggest:

— **Celebrate their life rather than focusing on their death.** Every soul comes into a physical incarnation wishing to leave the world a better place. Do something that will memorialize them for something they loved. If your relative was an avid bowler, for example, consider taking disadvantaged children to a day of bowling in his name, or sponsor a team where his name would be remembered in that manner.

— **Share funny stories.** Those who cross over are now experiencing being back in joy and would like nothing better than for you to feel that. Take a friend or another loved one out to a comedy show or funny movie and say that it is compliments of the deceased. On the way there or back, share funny stories about them. Get a notepad and write down a funny memory with them on each sheet. Place the slips in a jar and pick one out each day.

— **Start a foundation or raise money for one.** If your loved one had a favorite charity or cause, raise money in their name. Organize a walk, a bake sale, a block party, or even a family reunion where everyone who comes makes a video with a memory of the deceased and offers a donation to a charity in their name. You can also plant a tree in their name so that something lives on that you can visit.

The more things that you can do to keep the name and memory of your loved one alive, the more you will come to realize that they are still with you—just in another form. And if they could help to spread joy on the planet even after their exit, then they will still be growing both their soul's energy and yours!

There are some types of deaths that affect the hearts and minds of human beings in a very profound way because they are so hard to understand on a logical level. A very important question about one of those forms of death comes from *Audrey McNaughton,* a retired receptionist from St. Catharines, Ontario, who asks:

Can suicide be part of a life plan for soul lessons?

Generally, suicide takes place when a person reaches adult age, although in some instances it might happen when a child is experiencing severe trauma. It is not ever a part of the soul plan in the incarnation backstory. It occurs when the human is going through so much emotional pain and has lost so much soul energy that they feel there is no way that they can go on. Sometimes it is done when one feels that they are going to die anyway, and they take the death into their own hands.

I understand that many feel that suicide is a very individual and selfish decision. However, it actually is not. The person who contemplates suicide has some important things that are going on in the background. Remember that your brain is charged with, above all things, keeping your body alive. So when the brain comes to the determination that it would be in the best interest of the body to end its life, this means that the brain has decided it has no ability to stop any more soul loss, so the body and mind would continue to deteriorate. The soul consciousness now must decide whether it wants to go on with a steady decline and displaced soul energy or to support the brain's decision. Often the soul powering your body will want to stay in the hopes of changing the circumstances, and that is where the higher self comes in.

Gerry and I recently spoke about the suicide of a family member with a woman who was trying to understand it. An analogy came to me and I offered it. Please do not feel that I am making light of suicide in any way by using this analogy. I share it here as it did very much help the woman, and I feel at this time it may help many others as well.

If the situation of life were a baseball game, then the person contemplating suicide would be the pitcher. He has been doing pretty well in the game but lately has gotten into trouble, and no matter what he throws out there, he is getting hit. No matter how hard he tries, the situation keeps getting worse. The soul of the pitcher wants to stay in the game because he came to win, help his team be the best they could be, and bring great joy to the crowd. But now the crowd is booing, and things are looking bleak.

Now the coach (representing the higher self) comes to the mound. He addresses the pitcher, "Do you really believe you can pull yourself out of this? You have a choice. You could come out of the game now, and maybe give the team a chance to come back. I'm not complaining about how you played. You tried the best you could, but you took some bad hits, and some of them have really hurt you—even physically. You tried to come back from your injuries, you tried to play through the pain, but you just kept getting reinjured. And now your body is saying that it needs to retire. If you come out, there's no shame to it. We'll take you back and get you fixed up, and then you can have a start on another team. Maybe for the next team, we'll try to find you one that will give you a better chance to win. What do you think?"

Very often, that is the kind of behind-the-scenes conversation between the soul and the incarnated consciousness that causes it to decide to "retire." It is not about selfishness or cowardice. Even when it is a rash decision—perhaps a man in a police standoff, for example—it is a decision that the soul makes to end this incarnation in the same manner that it came in: by its own power. However, in no way am I trying to romanticize or encourage suicide. Trust me that no one makes that decision unless they can find no better option at that point.

Now there are times that a decision is not really thought out. When people die of overdoses of drugs, it is generally not a death wish. Many people who attempt to commit suicide change their mind when they begin, and the higher self may intercede when there is a clear-cut mistake. But when it is intentional and successful, then there is a bigger picture that the soul and the higher self has seen, and it is believed that it is in the best intention of those on the "team" of that person. Even in suicide, souls are seeking to ensure that the amount of sadness they create will not diminish the joy of other incarnated souls, and that they will not drag others down with them. The soul is always seeking to expand potential joy, as hard as that might be to understand.

So please share compassion and love for those who have come to that point where they have taken their lives. They are deserving of your love and compassion and even your gratitude.

∞

Another question about "untimely" death came from *Aimee Lorincz*, a mother of two young daughters from Tahoe, California. Amy wonders:

Why must young souls die? Why are some lives taken before they have ever had the chance to begin?

When you come into this lifetime, you choose your time and place and your family of birth, and then everything else from there, as I have said, is pure improvisation. But there are some instances where the higher self, within the overall backstory of the soul's creation, will leave open the possibility that this soul could make an early exit.

For example, a family may carry a recessive gene that allows a baby to be born, but to live for only a very short time. That experience will send ripples of energetic waves of love and compassion toward the parents and for the child. Although that life might be very short, the energy of love and compassion that they have produced are immense. In the same vein, there are times that a child may develop an illness when they are still very young, or they may die as a result of living in an abusive household. In this case, the higher self, in looking at the potential challenges of an incarnation, may take that risk in the planning, not knowing for certain whether the disease or abuse would take place. After all, there are many freewill decisions that could affect both. The results on a human level are sad and so emotionally damaging; but on a soul level, the sometimes worldwide outpouring of love increases the soul energy and shifts the travesty toward an energy of positive momentum. Please note that your soul will never exactly plan for this to happen. It is part of the random occurrences of free will.

Answers for questions like this are so hard, especially for things that happen to children, because you can't see the fact that they are going to be fine. The physical form is temporary. Even for us, who do understand it, to see these things happen brings no joy for us nor for your soul. But it is the nature of having a world where there is polarity, and the death of a child always brings to the world more resulting positive energy than negative—often simply from the outpouring of love for the lost little innocent. But the pain left behind is substantial. Please, dear ones, if this occurs in your life, remember those souls and you can help them to live on through their memory.

There is a growing, ongoing issue facing the aging bodies and souls on your planet. *Karen Gaynor,* a nanny for newborns and premature babies, asks:

When someone is afflicted with Alzheimer's to such a degree that they are comatose, where is their spirit? Someone once told me that my loved one was in between heaven and earth—not stuck, but sort of in and out, hopping back and forth.

When someone is in a comatose state, whether from Alzheimer's or another condition, the presence of soul that exists in the body may vary greatly. If your body is existing and breathing without outside life support, then this is an indication that there is soul energy still within the body. The body can exist with a very small amount of soul energy, and very often the predominant amount has returned to the higher self. So it is a fairly accurate description to say the soul is hopping in and out of the comatose body. It is much like the situation in pregnancy, in which a soul is testing the waters to see how much energy to invest. In the case of the comatose person, the soul is assessing whether the body has healed enough to support full consciousness.

A person often goes into a coma because of extreme physical trauma and resulting soul loss. In other words, it is determined that it would be better for the consciousness to not be in the body so that it is not experiencing extreme pain, or feeling trapped and powerless. You have all heard of cases in which someone will return from a coma years after entering one. In those rare instances, it is because the body has healed enough to allow full consciousness to enter, and it can now support it. Sometimes this will also be an opportunity for soul growth, both for the person in the coma and the people who love that person. The body does still continue to update and upload information to the higher self as long as natural breathing is taking place, so it is true that the person in the coma is always aware to an extent of what is happening around them.

On the topic of death and dying, it is inevitable that we will also cross the threshold into the nature of karma. One of the most interesting takes on the question came to us from *Kristine Thies*, who is on a voyage of self-discovery in Long Grove, Illinois. She asks:

> *If I do not resolve issues here on earth, will I have to come back to earth again and continue working on these issues? I don't want to! It's too painful and I can't control what another person thinks or feels about me. I think people should respect each other and agree to disagree through love. So whatever you can explain to me on this question would be very helpful!*

Dear one, by doing what you are doing, coming from a place of love and "agreeing to disagree," you are doing everything that you should to create the energy to allow your soul to expand. You do not need to concern yourself with how others in your life or relationships are reacting to your efforts to send love, compassion, and joy; you need merely to be doing so. If someone desires to reject or accept love, that is up to them. If your sending out of energy is rejected by the recipient, the energy will come to you in some other form.

Karma, however, is not a case of having to come back to take care of unfinished business from a previous life—it is not a makeup for a school lesson that you did not complete! Karma is about like energy attracting like energy—that is all! If you create a certain type of energy, then you will attract that energy back to you. It is all happening in the same lifetime. Yes, it is true that every lifetime has issues of karma, so some things may become part of your backstory more than once, as the nature of these issues cause them to repeat themselves. But life is not a school; it is an experience. And there is no way to get it wrong.

BREATH, CONNECTION, JOY, AND PLANETARY CHANGE

> *"You reverse problems in the world in the same manner that you reverse problems in your personal relationships: You do not take things personally, and you come from a place of compassion and love at all times."*

I have loved having the opportunity to answer your questions throughout this book. I know that sometimes, things that might normally seem so difficult are so much easier with just the slightest bit of direction. So let us look at some of the topics that we have explored thus far as a result of your queries.

First of all, you are a divine being who spans space and time. You place your energy in all types of life forms throughout the universe. When you entered this life form, you did so through breath, and it is breath that keeps energy moving through you in your lifetime. Breath is so crucial to your existence as a human, as without it, you go back to your spirit state. So in this interconnected universe, it makes sense that you would also learn what it is like to be a part of the life form that brings forth the very oxygen that allows you to breathe and that is part of the structure of the water that you need to drink in order to survive. I am speaking, of course, of the trees!

We have spoken so much in this book about how the understanding of the true nature of the soul energy and divinity of all things was so present in the belief systems of the original peoples of this planet, particularly in the shamans of those tribes. This concept of the sacredness of this planet and all of its life forms is not lost on **Denise Linn**, an internationally renowned spiritual teacher, founder of the International Institute of Soul Coaching®, and best-selling author of *Unlock the Secret Messages of Your Body!* and *Past Lives, Present Miracles.* Her work honors the elements, the power of nature, and the spirit of the planet. She has also helped us to share angelic information and has witnessed firsthand the miracles that occur when one opens up to infinite possibilities. She shares one of those stories:

Angels are only a breath away. Over the decades, I have taught many seminars about angels; I love teaching these courses because wondrous events often follow in their wake. For example, I was teaching a course about angels in Ireland to a group of 500 people. In one exercise I asked everyone to raise their right arm to send energy to others in the room.

In the center of the room was a man who was in a wheelchair due to a very serious, debilitating disease. He was dismayed that, because of his illness, he was unable to lift his arm; but he really wanted to send energy to others. Suddenly he felt someone from behind lift his arm. He assumed that one of seminar helpers was lifting his arm, but when he turned to see who it was to thank them . . . there was no one there! Remarkably, he could feel the fingers and hand of someone holding his arm up, and there was even an indentation in his arm where it was being held.

Five times I asked for participants to raise their arms, and five times the invisible hand lifted his arm. His wife, who sat next to him, also saw the indentations in his upper arm, as an unseen hand held his arm high. At the completion of the course, the couple came to me, their eyes streaming with tears. They knew that they'd witnessed a miracle.

But just as there are miracles that take place when someone taps into the energy of the angelic realm, there are miracles as well that happen when you tap into the elemental realm—the realm of all things that exist around you. The planet on which you live on a daily basis naturally provides enough food to nourish all of its inhabitants. It produces natural medicines to cure illness and even facilitates the sharing of energy. So I was excited to receive Denise's question, which allows me to expand on this information. She asks:

I love listening to the whispers and secret messages from the trees. Could you share about the deeper energy of trees on our planet? Thank you!

I love to speak of trees because in so doing I am paying homage to perhaps the most important player in the earth's ecosystem. In order for humans to have life, you must have breath. Breath carries energy into your body, and allows you to exhale stale energy and already-processed cells that are ready to be recycled. For this process, you need to have oxygen, and in order to have oxygen you need to have trees. In one of the most amazing feats of creation, trees were designed to store and convert carbon dioxide to oxygen, helping to clean both water and air.

In addition, trees are interconnected to each other through fungal networks that allow older and more established trees to "feed" smaller, less stable ones. In other words, trees have families and support their community in the same way as humans! This communication does not only occur on the fungal level. As trees are producing oxygen and releasing it into the atmosphere, they are also producing very gentle waves of air that rustle the branches and leaves. If I could give this particular process a name, I would refer to it as the "song of the trees." Mankind has tried to replicate this sound through the creation of woodwind instruments, such as the flute and the clarinet. The movement of the air produces a whistle, and the positioning of the branches of the tree and the leaves acts in the same manner as a person's fingers and the stops of the musical instrument.

With each breath that the tree releases into the environment, there is a story told of what is occurring on and below the surface of the planet. Many cultures called trees the "tall standing ones" and believed that they had great wisdom because they had seen so much and had learned to stay strong by swaying in the winds. If you take the time to be silent and listen to the sounds of the trees as they rustle and allow your mind to "imagine" what they are saying, you will be amazed at how your soul will help you to understand their message. You have placed some of your soul energy in the trees, and when the body allows the soul to listen, it will hear the soul in all things; you will hear the messages those souls are trying to bring. This is the skill of the shaman—to hear the messages of the soul in all things. That is also the basis of the word *namaste*, which translates as "my soul honors your soul." When you honor the soul in all things, then you will learn how to hear the messages they share. And when you identify yourself as being one with the planet on which you live, then you can begin to understand how to live in better harmony with both the planet and all its inhabitants.

Trees can also offer another wonderful service to the human race, which they already offer to many other species. They can transmute the negative energy that you are holding and breathe into you fresh, more grounded energy! Several years ago there was a movement to "hug a tree," and many people found that doing so left them feeling lighter and more refreshed. In fact, those who are not as protective of the earth often refer to those who are as "tree huggers." When you place your arms around a large tree (or your hands around a smaller one), the tree will draw from you the cells that are ready to be released and then return fresh energy to your body. This helps to make you feel more grounded and more balanced. It all comes down to a question of balance. The planet that you live on is always seeking to create balance, always seeking to find ways to repair itself and create new systems to respond to the needs of its inhabitants. All of you as human beings must remember to see yourself as "earth" beings that are just as much a part of the planet as the flowers that grow from the ground and the bees that pollinate those flowers.

◈

Just as the planet seeks to bring you balance, one of the most important things that your soul came to this earth to experience was the opportunity to find, or create, joy in everything! **Sonia Choquette**, a spiritual teacher, six-sensory consultant, and best-selling author of *Grace, Guidance, and Gifts* and *Traveling at the Speed of Love,* shares a wonderful and personal story about the miracles that happen when you don't lose sight of the simple things that bring you joy. She shares her story here:

I met my own guardian angel many years ago. I'd retreated to Hawaii in the dead of winter to recuperate from a long and exhausting bout of sleep deprivation after the birth of my two-in-a-row babies, a never-ending house renovation, and overwhelming appointments. For the first several days after I arrived all I did was sleep, but on the third day I roused myself and went down to the beach, where I sat quietly near the water reflecting on my life.

Although I had two beautiful daughters and a wonderful husband, I wasn't happy. Our lives were stretched far too thin, we were over our heads in debt, and all Patrick and I did was fight. Having very little outside support at the time, both my husband and I were overwhelmed with responsibility. It was painfully clear that all of the joy had drained away from our lives, and we were merely surviving from day to day.

As I sat on the beach, far away from it all, I prayed for a change—something to get my life back on track.

The following day, I strolled along the beach for an hour or so, then spontaneously turned and wandered toward the city to explore. I entered a metaphysical bookstore with the feeling that I'd been led there. There was a single woman working behind the counter as I began to browse, and I found myself feeling grateful that she seemed preoccupied so that I could wander around without interruption.

After a few minutes, a very beautiful African man walked from the back room and directly toward me. He was about 6'2" and dressed in all white, with a gorgeous smile and twinkling laugh. The minute he saw me he said, "Hello. I've been waiting for you."

"Me?" I asked, surprised.

"Yes," he answered, as he motioned me over to a bin of spiritual posters. "Look here," he said, pulling out a poster of a female angel collapsed on the beach. "This is you."

"Very perceptive," I laughed. "I do feel like that right now."

"Now look here," he continued. "This is what you must do." He pulled out another poster, this time of a male angel embracing the female angel and flying toward heaven. I suddenly felt a sad twinge of pain, realizing how far apart Patrick and I had drifted. We were both working so much that we rarely saw each other anymore, and when we did we were hardly in the mood to listen to each other or spend time together. To top it all off, neither of us had any time to ourselves, let alone the opportunity to enjoy our daughters.

"Connect with your partner and remember to dance," the man said, smiling as he turned around one last time and said, "I will be back."

I stood there holding the two posters, puzzling over what he'd just said, when the woman behind the counter asked me if I needed help. "No, thank you," I answered. "The gentleman in the back room has helped me quite a bit already."

She frowned and said, "Gentleman? What gentleman?"

"The one who just walked into the back room," I answered.

Shaking her head at me as though I were nuts, she said, "There's no one else working here." After ducking into the back room to check for herself, she emerged, still shaking her head, and reaffirmed, "There's no one there."

Confused, I looked at the two posters. Then I remembered the man's shimmering all-white outfit, and I knew in an instant that he was an angel . . . my angel. He had stepped in out of nowhere to bring me the message to relax, simplify my life, enjoy Patrick and the girls, and trust that everything would be all right—a message that I desperately needed to hear just then. Because he said he'd be back, I knew in my heart that my family and I would be helped. I was finally able to smile, then laughed out loud as a wonderful feeling of reassurance swept over me.

"Never mind," I said to the woman as I slowly walked outside, shocked at what had just happened, and nearly delirious with relief. I was so grateful that this entity had shown up to brighten my dreary life that day. From that moment on, I called my guardian angel "Bright."

The purpose of this last chapter is twofold: (1) to leave you with a sense of hope and the realization that there is no reason why you should not have an undying sense of optimism, and (2) to help you know how to plant the seeds to a brighter tomorrow! Love, security, peace, and well-being are things that start at home. They are feelings that start in your heart and expand outward to your relationship, your family, your friends, and finally to the other people in the world who will be impacted by what you believe, who you are, and how you act.

In Sonia's story, the physical manifestation of an angelic energy came to her not to discuss what she needed to do in order to save the world but to save her relationship with her husband—and herself, too! As large as your soul may be, and as large as the universe may be, your relationship with your angel is totally one-on-one. When I explain the vastness of all that you touch, it may be hard to understand that at the same time there is such an incredible intimacy that exists between all of these different levels of creation. The message that Sonia's angel brought to her is the same message for all of you that read this: Relax, simplify, enjoy, and trust and know that you are not powerless!

At the same time that I am urging you to expand your capacity for joy and optimism, you unfortunately need only turn on the news to find things going on in the world that have the potential to pull your energy down. Sonia reflects on this:

How do we remain filled with confidence and love in our hearts when the world seems so dark with terrorism and hate-filled atrocities between groups of people that appear to be growing in so many parts of the world? How can a person help reverse this downward spiral of consciousness happening now?

As simplistic an answer as this might seem, you reverse problems in the world in the same manner that you reverse problems in your personal relationships: You do not take things personally, and you come from a place of compassion and love at all times.

Imagine for a moment that you are on a track team, and you are one of the runners that must jump over hurdles. This is a skill that must be developed over time, because in order to clear the hurdles at high speed, you will need to develop balance, grace, and the ability to get "lift." If you are the type of person who makes assumptions about the hurdles in front of you, then you might "jump to conclusions" and reach the wrong height. Perhaps you are truly able to jump over any obstacle in front of you but you don't really think that you have this talent, so you "drag your feet behind you" and find yourself tripping over the obstacles. Some think the best idea is to just go around the obstacles, but that means leaving your lane and going into someone else's and following their path for a while until you think it's safe to go back to yours.

The successful runner pays no attention to the runners next to them. Their race is against themselves and their own personal obstacles. They run at the obstacles with joy and abandon; they know that they will clear these hurdles because they have successfully cleared hurdles all of their lives. The runner isn't distressed by jumping to a conclusion or tripping over their own feet, because they can correct that at the next hurdle. And in the end it is not about the competition with the other runners, it is about the run. It is about clearing the obstacles with the confidence that comes from past success.

Life is not about the race, and it is not about the lessons. It is about the experience, and the experience you seek and the energy you wish to bring to the world is joy!

The world has always been full of problems and there have always been those who, from the place of their own sense of powerlessness, have terrorized or bullied others. Plato, the ancient Greek philosopher, wrote the following in *The Republic,* and it still holds true today: "When the mind's eye rests on objects illuminated by truth and reality, it understands and comprehends them, and functions intelligently; but when it turns to the twilight world of change and decay, it can only form opinions, its vision is confused and its beliefs shifting, and it seems to lack intelligence." Clearly the world in which you live has seen these same problems for quite a while if they came to Plato's attention; and your history books are full of stories of those who have committed terrible atrocities and others who have acted with transcendent heroism. Which side of the experience you decide to focus on will determine your sense of reality in the creation of the *global energy*. And make no mistake: your thoughts and the thoughts of others are creating the global energy.

In order to stay filled with confidence and allow yourself to always come from a place of love and compassion in your heart, you have to illuminate the truth and reality of knowing what you now know about the soul. You now know the truth that you are all the same energy, and this energy is playing a different role in this lifetime than someone else may be playing. You also know the truth that you are eternal, so whatever happens here is just a part of a much bigger story that you have agreed to be a part of. But most important, you have learned that you can *choose joy!* You can choose to not focus on the change and decay of the world, and instead focus on finding out about the wonderful things that are happening.

Find positive, or at least balanced, sources of news from the world that will allow you to truly understand the beliefs of different cultures and realize that for every different group there are angels who are communicating with them and attempting to spread messages of love. So do not pray for the decline of a group or a culture; instead, pray for there to be angels surrounding them and lifting their vibration to a higher place of love. You can do this!

The only way to elevate the energy of hate and violence and fear is with love and gentleness, faith and trust. If you are constantly living your life from this place, even if you are not focused on world events, you are creating a positive energy that is going out into the world and changing it.

∽

This brings us then to what I think is the perfect place to close this chapter. One of the letters we received was written almost as though it could have been sent from your higher self, seeking to reassure you. Intuitive coach *Kristen Barrett Mattern* of Santa Cruz, California, shares the following:

> *I realize there are as many differing views and opinions as there are people on the earth. I hear many people say that the world needs saving from human destruction. The world needs more love. Save the children, save the whales, etc. I hear older people say that everything is worse—the economy, pollution, crime. They say we've lost our innocence as a society. Since I've been aware enough to think about these things, I have felt deep in my being that all is well with our world. I have felt that this physical environment is full of contrast, which gives us so much to experience. I feel that the so-called problems in the world are opportunities for individuals to experience true love—giving and receiving. When someone or something is helped or improved, they experience the receiving of love, and life is improved for them. The helper experiences love by fulfilling his or her purpose—by giving love. I feel that the world is expanding as naturally as the universe allows. I do not worry.*

To my dearest Kristen and to all of you other dear ones who are reading this book, *all is well with the world!* It is so hard for you, while in your physical condition and vibration, to realize that everything that exists around you has been *created* by you, and those around you! Much like a roller coaster, you are in the midst of a ride you have decided to take, which will thrill you, frighten you, take you to amazing heights, drop you from those heights without warning, make you laugh and scream, make you cry and be sick. And when it is over, and you are able to leave the ride and run trembling to the safety of a loved one's arms, you will look back over your shoulder at that ride and say, "I want to go on again!"

Such is the nature of your soul, which I hope you now better understand.

Let us now consider this wonderful world and the container that you have chosen to inhabit your physical world. For every news story that you hear of a person performing an atrocity, there are several million who are caring for their families, loving their wife or husband or girlfriend or boyfriend, watching their children play soccer, and leaving their hearts open to joy. If you could see your evolution from our point of view, you would see why we feel that you are heading toward, and for that matter are already within, a very bright future!

As you turn these final pages, let me just remind you that the truths that were brought forth in these chapters were the result of *your* questions, just as truth and beauty and joy always comes to the surface as a result of your primary question as a soul, which is always: "How Can I Be More Happy?"

These are some of my very simple suggestions as to how to help that happen. They are actions you can take that will help you *feel* for yourselves the energetic answers to many of these questions you've asked herein:

Love, laugh, share.

Keep your head up and smile.

Throw your shoulders back to open your heart center.

Sing, dance, and do joyful exercise.

Hug an animal.

Hug a person.

Say "Why is my life so joyful" at least three times a day.

Do something you loved when you were a child.

Do something naughty and playful.

Give thanks for all you have.

Celebrate another's success.

Remember the people who have challenged you with fondness.

Remember the ones who loved you with fondness as well.

Hug yourself.

Forgive someone and stop judging anyone—especially yourself.

Pray for an enemy to find joy and love in their heart.

And never forget, whenever you need help . . .

Call on a Legion of Angels!

Go in peace, dear ones!
All my love,

Margaret

ACKNOWLEDGMENTS

When I wrote the Acknowledgments for my first book, *Messages from Margaret,* I found it really hard to know where to stop. That's one of the wonderful things that happens when you get into a space of gratitude: you just want to keep going. So be forewarned—this may take a while!

I dedicated my first book to a wonderful woman, and often during my radio show and in the majority of my personal conversations, you will hear me speak about Gail. The Gail that I am speaking of is Gail Lisa. We met in 1988, and from that first conversation I knew that my soul longed to be with her—and now, 27 years later, nothing has changed. Gail, you live your life with the goal of bringing joy to, and taking care of, others. When my mom became ill and could no longer live on her own, you left your job to help care for her. You became the one she always called upon because your kindness always shone through. You loved David, the little autistic boy whom you were volunteering with, so much that he grew by leaps and bounds—and you wound up taking him into our home permanently! You are the one who brings beauty and love to our home—wisdom, joy, and an appropriate amount of silliness—always seeking to live truthfully and helping everyone learn to "follow their bliss!" You are an amazing mother, an even more amazing grandmother, the best friend any human or animal could have, my greatest inspiration, my toughest and yet most caring critic, my love, and my partner in life! With all of the gratitude one can feel, I dedicate all that I am and all that I do to you! Thank you so very much for sharing your life with me and for being you! I will always love you and be your biggest fan, and you will always be the wind beneath Margaret's wings. She asked me to say thank you, and I love you as well!

You hear Margaret speak quite a bit about joy in this book and about raising your level of joy. For me, family has always been a great source of joy. Through meeting Gail I had the opportunity to become part of an expanded family, and I will tell you more about them in a bit. But my original family began with two amazing daughters—Melissa and Tiffany! Each of them brings their talents and love to the world in their own special way, usually involving creativity, being of service to others, and dancing to the music of their own unique drummers. I am so incredibly proud of both of you, and I thank you for always being supportive of me—even in some really tough times! I love how the free-flowing "hippie chick" still lives on in your hearts as you have transitioned into amazing women.

Tiff, I love and support how passionate you are about life and how you aren't afraid to be a vocal advocate for changes that would allow everyone to control the destiny of their own bodies. At the same time, I am so proud of how you strive for excellence in all that you do—at work, at home, and in your education. You are the most determined woman I have ever met. But through all of that seriousness you are loving, funny, and inviting, and a wonderful wife, mother, daughter, and friend to others. You were also my first Girl Scout, little valentine and actually my first editor! You will always be my favorite concert companion and bartender!

As a firstborn, Tiff was a tough act to follow, but that's exactly what Melissa did. She brought with her different gifts, which are affecting the world in equally powerful ways. Lissa, you are one of the most artistic and creative people that I ever met, and everything you do is filled with such love and caring—from Halloween costumes to cupcakes to beautiful personalized gifts—they all touch the hearts of those around you. You are a tireless advocate for autistic children and their parents and a welcome addition to the social-service efforts at your church. I could not get a newsletter out without your technical expertise, and while you are always trying to bring some heaven to people's lives, you are also funny as hell!

I love both of you dearly, and especially how you not only do these things, but teach them to new generations as well. And so to my grandchildren, Ian, Ryan, and Kyla, I have these words that I want to be remembered here so that someday you can look back and recall some wonderful things about yourselves.

Ian, you have already stood in protest lines with your mom and been willing to be the younger generation's voice for many causes. You advocate peace and love, and you grow more handsome and intelligent every day. You have an ear for music and a heart for it as well! Remember that, despite what your teachers may tell you, life *wasn't* meant to be a struggle. And the more love, ease, peace, and just being *you* that you bring to life, the happier you will be and the more joy you will bring to others. Whatever you do, just keep Grandpa away from the windows on the ferry! ☺ I love you!

Ryan, you may not completely understand why you chose to come into the seeming limitations of your autism, but one thing is for sure: you never stop amazing us with the barriers you break through. And the pure love and gentle nature that shines through you touches our hearts and souls! You give us all the chance to see the world through your eyes, and it gives us the opportunity to see how truly wonderful life is! Someday, thinking about Mr. Bear and "head bonking" while we say "I love you" may be a distant memory in your mind—but this loving memory will always be in my heart and bring a tear to my eye. I love you!

Kyla is an energetic cheerleader, gymnast, and dancer who aspires to have her own YouTube channel—look out for it! But it is your kind heart, Kyla, which makes me equally proud! At the tender age of six, you saw the struggles of homeless kids and asked your mom to help you start www.kylakares.org, a nonprofit that offers backpacks filled with wonderful things for homeless and displaced children to help them to feel a little more at home—wherever they might have to be. I wish we could take that love in your heart and put it in a backpack for everyone! I love you!

There is a prayer that Melissa says every night with her children that ends "I am smart, I am kind, I am caring, and I am going to change the world!" I love that prayer. Gail, my grandkids' adopted grandma, so loved that prayer when Kyla said it at our home that she started to say it with her grandkids, Max and Sarah.

Max is a wiz at math and a budding country guitar player. He may wind up becoming a professional soccer player—yes he is that good! Max, you are learning—and loving—to be a gentleman through and through. Always stay that way, as a true gentleman brings peace and caring to the world. I will always remember your trusting me to help you with math homework—and somehow our still getting it right! I so admire how you have reinvented yourself: from being a shy young boy to being so outgoing and willing to reach out to make friends with everyone. And your heart is as big as your smile! Keep loving life, playing hard, and being you!

Sarah loves to dance and sing and write her own songs; and she plays piano like she had lessons in the womb! She loves girly things and tomboy things and life and laughter—and she loves to bring that joy to others. She often watches me and "journeys" with me when I do shamanic work, and I know that as the years go on she is going to grow into her intuitive gifts. We call you "Princess Golden-Heart" for a reason, Sarah; please always let that heart glow with love. I am so honored that both you and Max adopted me and call me grandpa! You two have the most contagious laughs that bring joy to everyone, and I love you both!

I would be remiss if I did not send a shout-out to the men behind these wonderful women and grandchildren. So to Ian's dad, John Greene; Kyla and Ryan's dad, David Medina; and Max and Sarah's dad, Efren Cifuentes, and their stepdad, Gurkan Unal, to you is entrusted the job of being the anchor in your children's lives and supporting their moms in caring for them and teaching them by your example. It is important to teach them that dads love as deeply and spiritually and joyfully as moms, and I love and honor your role in teaching them that lesson. You are all good men—who are always seeking to be better men—and that is awesome. I love you guys!

Now back to the ladies! You can't become an adopted grandpa unless you become an adopted dad; and Gail's daughters, Amanda and Courtney, bestowed exactly that honor on me! You adopted me into your lives and allowed me to share your teenage years and your young adulthood, then gave me the ultimate honor of being the person you chose to officiate at your weddings.

Acknowledgments

Amanda, you have always been a seeker and always sought your own unique path in the world. I have always loved your natural curiosity about everything and everyone. I learned all of my interviewing skills listening to you in conversations with others around the dining room table! While it perhaps made for some fancy logistics, I was so honored to have the chance to walk you down the aisle at your wedding and then slide on over to perform the ceremony. You are so strong and willing to take on whatever life confronts you with and turn it into something good. You're smart and organized, and you will always succeed at whatever you attempt! I love how you stand up for Max and Sarah, and they always know you have their back! Remember always that life loves you and that, in the words of the magnet on your mom's fridge, the world is conspiring in your favor! I love you!

Courtney, you are bright, talented, and creative. Who else but you could manage to create the wonderful Annual Parties at the farm and to make each one bigger, better, grander, and always more fun! They have become legendary! You have mastered the art of manifestation and draw to you the most amazing experiences and opportunities! Even as a child, you were always at the center of your friends and that still continues to this day. You love to spread joy and to make sure that everyone celebrates life! You are always the one discovering new and fun things to do and then inviting everyone you know to join in. For that reason you have brought to you the most amazing and eclectic group of friends, all of whom hold one thing in common—they love being with you! As do your mom and I! Thank you for always spreading your joy in our direction and for helping to lift the vibration of all those in your life! Life loves you because you love life—and I love you too!

And to the two other men that were adopted into this family along with me—Vincent Emmolo and Gurkan Unal—I'm glad you joined the team! You are both really good men, and I'm proud to think of you, alongside John and David, as my sons. Gurkan, I appreciate and honor how you love and care for Amanda and the children, and how great you are at making everyone feel so special! Vinny, you always bring joy with you when you walk into a room, and I love how you have reached out to Margaret for automotive and business coaching! Thanks to you both for sharing beers, laughter, stories, and good times! I love you guys!

Earlier, I mentioned the amazing young man named David who entered our lives when he was only 4½ and came to live with us for good when he was just 10. David Anderson is, as of the writing of this book, 24 years old. He was unable to speak when we met him, yet has progressed and gone on to graduate from high school. Our lives, as well as the lives of the animals on our little horse farm, are so much the better because of him! He has a wicked sense of humor; an uncanny ability to mimic the voices of almost every cartoon character; a unique artistic perspective that allows him to create beautiful, gentle, and original cartoon characters; and a heart and sensitivity that always looks out for other people. David, you are the foreman of our farm, but you are the caretaker of everyone's hearts—and nobody could do that job better than you!

I am fortunate to have my brothers George Gavin and Jim Cramer living pretty close to me. But even if there were a physical distance between us, we would still be close. They are both amazing men! When he was in his early forties, my brother George suffered a series of major strokes that left him paralyzed throughout many parts of his body and took away his ability to speak—which, for someone who loves to talk, was the hardest part I think. But George is a fighter and took back his ability to speak not just English but also the six other languages he knew. He also regained his mobility while never losing his zest for life. He went on to become a minister to other stroke victims; they would rally because his personal story gave them hope and fight! Every day of his life is filled with gratitude for being here and a desire to spread love and joy to others! I am so proud of you and love you so, my brother!

When George was lying in that hospital bed, it was his partner Jim that was always there! Jim is another one of our adopted family members, and personally I think that there could never have been a better addition. He is an amazing cook—the kind that could be on one of those reality cooking programs—and also a gifted business-man who manages with purpose and compassion. But what always touches me about Jim is that he forgets nothing important. There is never a birthday, special occasion, or an opportunity to show someone that they are loved that Jim doesn't remember and act upon. Jim, you have brought so much love to our family, and I couldn't love you more, my brother, even if you had been part of the family when we were younger! I am so grateful that we all have you in our lives!

Speaking of people who should be in reality cooking programs, my love and thanks go out to Barry and Jean Yurkiewicz, brother and sister-in-law and the two people who should have been voted "people you most want to invite you to dinner"! Barry is the chef and Jean the baker, and their kitchen is always filled with recipes I would never think to make—as well as funny conversation. Barry also acts as my "unofficial agent," telling anyone who might seem open to it about my writing and my work with Margaret. Thanks for your faith in me, your support of me, and your feeding of me! I love you both!

Since I wrote *Messages from Margaret,* there have been a number of people in our lives that made the transition to reconnect with their higher selves. I call upon them all the time when I am doing soul retrieval work, with the request of helping me to be successful in that endeavor, and I always feel that they are there when I call. To my brother Tom Gavin; his lovely wife, Judi; my good friend and "brother" Ted Yurkiewicz; and to my good friends and in-laws Tom and Doris O'Donnell, thank you for being open to and being so supportive of the work I do with Margaret. I know that we are all being supported by you daily and that your love surrounds all of us. And I know that my mom and dad, Tom Gavin, Sr., and Juliette Gavin; Gail's mom, Dot Yurkiewicz; and my girls' mom, Barbara, were there to welcome you and show you the ropes! Thanks to all of you!

This book would not have been possible if it were not for some wonderful people who participated in asking the compelling questions that allowed Margaret to craft what I hope will be a pretty good handbook for life.

First, my heartfelt thanks and deepest of gratitude to the wonderful authors who gave their time and thought and support to this book. Your questions were so very personal and powerful, and I am so deeply honored that you chose to be a part of it. Deep thanks to Arielle Ford, Kris Carr, John Holland, Nick Ortner, Meggan Watterson, Denise Linn, Sonia Choquette, Mike Dooley, Colette Baron-Reid, Sandra Anne Taylor, Pam Grout, Noah St. John, Jessica Ortner, Mona Lisa Schulz, Karen Noé, Barbara Carrellas, Christine Kloser, Jennifer Kass, davidji, and Anita Moorjani. Special thanks to John Holland for taking me under his wing at my first Hay House I Can Do It event, introducing me to everyone, and really helping me to feel like one of the Hay House "family." I am truly honored to call you my friend.

When I reached out through my e-mail list and my Hay House radio program to listeners and friends of Margaret who might want to submit questions for the book, I never expected the response that we received. Hundreds of e-mails came in every day with each question as powerful as the next. In the end, after numerous consultations with Margaret, we narrowed it down to just 33 of your wonderful wonderings. To all of you who submitted questions—I cannot thank you enough! And to those who made it into this book—the world thanks you as well! My deepest gratitude to Carina Rubin, Marilyn Enness, Mandi Morrissey, Laura Botsford, Jill Lebeau, Andrea Mueller, Tony Lauria, Katrin Navessi, Louis Szabo, Stella Hu, Cherie Ninomlya, Tina Sanchoo, Tiffany Nightingale, Tessa Sayers, Amanda Bingham, Lisbeth Hansen, Michelle Edinburg, Leslie Keith, Linda Crea, Danielle Lewis, Alejandra Kate, Indya Roberts, Niki Zamora, Leonarda Scandurra, Stephanie Tran, Audrey McNaughton, Aimee Lorincz, Karen Gaynor, Kristine Thies, Sharon Duquette, and Kristen Barrett Mattern. Special thanks to Kristen Willeumier and Bailey Jay for bringing down-to-earth spirituality, compassion, and lightness to their work—and for honoring me by their support of my work with Margaret!

I give thanks to my very good friends, both new and old, who have offered me so much love and support in so many ways. To my longest friend, Mike Carluccio, for taking my sandwiches in high school, which led us into a lifelong friendship. To James Malaniak for bringing "Love, Appreciate, Forgive" into this world and his friendship into my life, and teaching me that everything really is perfect all the time. To Jill Mangino for being such a great friend and for helping so many of us to "get the word out"! I know, Jill, that your time in the spotlight is about to happen too. And to Don Burkett and Preston "PJ" Bergen for being my personal "angels" that helped me get all of this started.

To my buddies at Hay House Radio, who do such an amazing job of helping all of us to create good radio and make it so easy! Diane Ray, thank you for heading up this wonderful team and for your voice and vision. To Mike Joseph, Joe Coburn, Rocky George III, Steve Morris, and Mitch Wilson, thank you for making on-air sound so professional and off-air so much fun! I love being a part of this team!

And of course, to the rest of the team at Hay House. My thanks go out to Louise Hay for being the visionary to create this transformative company and who still brings us inspiration by living the life she teaches. To Margarete Nielsen for aiding her in managing a company with so many moving parts—in such a gentle and caring manner. Christy Salinas for her amazing creative direction, Nick C. Welch for the interior layout and design, and Gaelyn Larrick for the beautiful cover artwork. To the wonderful marketing team at Hay House, especially Heather Tate, Tiffini Alberto, and Aurora Rosas. To the events team for all that you do, especially Mollie Langer and Adrian Sandoval, in making the ICDIs and other events so special for authors and attendees alike. To the wonderful team that brings us the Hay House World Summit, especially Jenele Lee. To our amazing web team, especially Kate Riley. To Alexandra Gruebler, Monica Meehan, and Anthony Bird for helping to get Margaret's words out to other countries throughout the world. To my publicist, Amanda Smith, and to all the sales and accounting and business staff that work so hard to help this company to be the success that it is. Thanks to Patty Gift for having the vision to choose the wonderful books that you bring to the world. Alex Freemon, my senior editor, I thank you for all of your support in pulling together the various pieces of getting this book to press—and I thank you especially for teaming me up with my editor, Nicolette Salamanca Young! Nikki, you were amazing to work with! You helped me to restructure content to make it flow more easily—to keep direction and focus—and you did so with caring, flexibility, support, and humor! Thank you for your excitement, encouragement, and gentle nudging, and for making the process fun. Thanks as well for all the cool computer tricks you taught me and all the other things that you researched and helped with! Margaret and I both also thank you for your uncanny ability to bring our very distinct voices so clearly to this book!

This brings me to another person at Hay House who started the process of bringing Margaret's voice and my voice out to the world—the CEO, Reid Tracy. Reid, you urged me to give Margaret a "voice" and to channel her live. You trusted bringing *Messages from Margaret* to the world, you trusted bringing us both to the radio—and you trusted in a letter from Margaret, helped formulate this current book, then reached out to many of the Hay House family to see if they would like to join us in this collaborative undertaking. You are never too busy to offer your guidance, support, and encouragement, and I am so very grateful for all that you have done—as is Margaret! Thank you so very much!

To Wayne Dyer for teaching me so much through the years by way of your books and PBS specials. It was wonderful to get to meet up with you, twice, in elevators at the ICDI events. I think now how coincidental that was—as you were responsible for elevating all of us to greater places!

Last but not least: thank you, Margaret, for sharing all of your wisdom with not only the world but me as well. You have changed my life, and I so look forward to the new adventures this book and you will bring us!

I hope that I have remembered everyone—but please know that if I went on to thank all of you who touch my heart, it would be a book in itself!

All my love,
Gerry

ABOUT THE
CONTRIBUTORS

Anita Moorjani was born in Singapore of Indian parents, and has lived in Hong Kong most of her life. She had been working in the corporate world for many years before being diagnosed with cancer in 2002. After falling into a coma in 2006, Anita entered into another realm where she experienced great clarity and insight on her life and purpose on earth. She experienced a remarkable recovery and shared her insights and story of healing in the *New York Times* bestseller *Dying to Be Me*, which has sold over one million copies worldwide and been translated into 42 languages.

Following the success of her book, Anita has been interviewed on primetime shows all over the world, including *Anderson Cooper 360, Fox News, The Jeff Probst Show,* the *Today* show, *Paranatural* on the National Geographic Channel, *The Pearl Report* in Hong Kong, and *Head Start with Karen Davila* in the Philippines. She travels the globe speaking at conferences.

Website: www.anitamoorjani.com

Arielle Ford is a leading personality in the personal growth and contemporary spirituality movement. For the past 25 years, she has been living, teaching, and promoting consciousness through all forms of media. She is a relationship expert, speaker, blogger for the *Huffington Post,* and the producer and host of Evolving Wisdom's Art of Love series.

Arielle is a gifted writer and the author of ten books, including the international bestseller *The Soulmate Secret: Manifest the Love of Your Life with the Law of Attraction* and her most recent *Turn Your Mate into Your Soulmate* (HarperElixir).

She has been called the "Cupid of Consciousness" and the "Fairy Godmother of Love." She lives in La Jolla, California, with her husband/soulmate Brian Hilliard and their feline friends.

Websites: www.MateToSoulmate.com and www.ArielleFord .com.

≈

Barbara Carrellas is a sex educator, sex/life coach, workshop facilitator, university lecturer, motivational speaker, and theater artist. She is the author of *Urban Tantra: Sacred Sex for the Twenty-First Century, Ecstasy Is Necessary: A Practical Guide,* and *Luxurious Loving.* Barbara is the founder of Urban Tantra®, an approach to sacred sexuality that adapts and blends a wide variety of conscious sexuality practices from Tantra to BDSM; and the co-founder of Erotic Awakening, a groundbreaking series of workshops focusing on the physical, spiritual, and healing powers of sex. Barbara's pioneering Urban Tantra® workshops were named best in New York City by *TimeOut/ New York* magazine. Barbara is a graduate of the Coney Island Sideshow School with a double major in snake handling and fire eating.

Website: www.barbaracarrellas.com

≈

Christine Kloser, "The Transformation Catalyst®" has trained nearly 70,000 entrepreneurs, authors, and leaders from more than 100 countries, and is well-recognized as the creative visionary behind the Transformational Author Experience® and Get Your Book Done®.

Whether through private mentoring, intimate retreats, live events, platform speaking, or global virtual training programs, Christine's students feel seen, heard, understood, valued, and transformed in ways they never thought possible. As a result they take action, claim their worth, write their books, experience life-changing breakthroughs, and fulfill their heart's calling.

Websites: www.ChristineKloser.com and www.Transformational Author.com

≈

Colette Baron-Reid is the author of *Remembering the Future, Messages from Spirit,* and *The Map,* published in 27 languages; *Wisdom of the Oracle Divination Cards;* and *The Wisdom of Avalon, Wisdom of the Hidden Realms,* and *The Enchanted Map* oracle card decks. She's an internationally acclaimed intuition expert and psychic medium, known affectionately by her clients as "The Oracle," and she stars in the hit Canadian TV show *Messages from Spirit with Colette Baron-Reid.* Originally from Toronto, Colette lives in Connecticut with her husband and two poms. Tune in to Hay House Radio for her weekly call-in show *Ask the Oracle.*

Website: www.colettebaronreid.com

davidji is an internationally recognized mind-body health and wellness expert, mindful performance trainer, meditation teacher, and best-selling author of *destressifying: The Real-World Guide to Personal Empowerment, Lasting Fulfillment, and Peace of Mind;* and *Secrets of Meditation: A Practical Guide to Inner Peace and Personal Transformation,* winner of the Nautilus Book Award. He is credited with creating the 21-day meditation process, which spawned hundreds of 21-day meditation experiences and challenges around the world. Often referred to as the "Velvet Voice of Stillness," he can be heard on more than 500 guided meditations, available on iTunes, Amazon .com, HayHouse.com, Google Play, Spotify, Pandora, SoundCloud, and davidji.com. Each week, he hosts *LIVE from the SweetSpot* on HayHouseRadio.com.

Join the davidji SweetSpot Community at www.davidji.com.

Denise Linn's personal journey began as a result of a near-death experience at age 17. Her life-changing experiences and remarkable recovery set her on a spiritual quest that led her to explore the healing traditions of many cultures, including those of her own Cherokee ancestors. Denise also lived in a Zen Buddhist monastery for more than two years.

Denise is an internationally renowned teacher in the field of self-development. She's the author of the bestseller *Sacred Space* and the award-winning *Feng Shui for the Soul,* and has written 18 books, which are available in 29 languages.

Website: www.DeniseLinn.com

≈

Jennifer Kass's mission is to make love a global force, awakening all willing hearts and minds to create a world that works for everyone. In the past five years, Jennifer has mentored hundreds one-one-one all over the world in her transformational programs, created the #LOVEPIONEER app and the weekly *Love Pioneer* podcast, and speaks to audiences on the power of transformative love.

Website: www.jenniferlkass.com

≈

Jessica Ortner is the *New York Times* best-selling author of *The Tapping Solution for Weight Loss & Body Confidence.* After opting out of college, she began interviewing leaders in innovation and success in order to create her own path. She has conducted over 600 interviews since 2007. Jessica teamed up with her brother Nick Ortner to produce the breakthrough documentary film on EFT/Meridian Tapping, *The Tapping Solution.* Jessica hosts the Tapping World Summit, an annual online event that has attracted more than 1,000,000 attendees from around the world.

Website: www.TheTappingSolution.com

≈

John Holland, the author of *The Spirit Whisperer, Born Knowing, Psychic Navigator, 101 Ways to Jump-Start Your Intuition,* and *Power of the Soul,* among other works, is an internationally renowned psychic medium who's been lecturing, demonstrating, and reading for private clients for almost two decades. He has been featured on The History Channel's *Psychic History, Unsolved Mysteries, Extra,* and the A&E special *Mediums: We See Dead People.* He also has a popular weekly call-in radio show, *Spirit Connections,* on HayHouseRadio.com.

Website: www.johnholland.com

≈

Karen Noé is a psychic medium and the author of *The Rainbow Follows the Storm, Through the Eyes of Another,* and *Your Life After Their Death.* She is the founder of the Angel Quest Center in Ramsey, New Jersey, where she teaches classes, gives readings, and practices alternative healing. You can listen to Karen on *The Angel Quest Radio Show* by tuning to www.wrcr.com on the first Saturday of every month.
Website: www.karennoe.com

≈

Kris Carr is a multi-week *New York Times* best-selling author, speaker, and wellness activist. She is the subject and director of the documentary *Crazy Sexy Cancer,* which premiered at the SXSW Film Festival and aired on TLC, the Discovery Channel, and The Oprah Winfrey Network. Kris is also the author of the award-winning Crazy Sexy book series. Her latest books, *Crazy Sexy Diet, Crazy Sexy Kitchen,* and *Crazy Sexy Juice,* will change the way you live, love, and eat! Kris regularly lectures at hospitals, wellness centers, corporations such as Whole Foods, and Harvard University. Named a "new role model" by *The New York Times,* she has been featured in *Glamour, Vanity Fair, Scientific American, Success, Forbes, People, Good Morning America,* the *Today* show, *CBS Evening News, The Early Show, Access Hollywood, The Doctors, Super Soul Sunday,* and *The Oprah Winfrey Show.* As an irreverent foot soldier in the fight against disease, Kris inspires countless people to take charge of their health and happiness by adopting a plant-passionate diet, self-care practices, and learning to live and love like they really mean it. In Oprah's words, "Kris Carr's riveting journey started a revolution."
Visit her at Kriscarr.com.

≈

Meggan Watterson is an author, speaker, and scholar of the divine feminine who inspires seekers to live from the audacity and authenticity of their soul. Her first book, *REVEAL: A Sacred Manual for Getting Spiritually Naked,* was described as "ignited prayer" by Eve Ensler, "life-changing" by Dr. Christiane Northrup, and "a blessing to the world" by Gabrielle Bernstein. Meggan's most recent book is titled *How to Love Yourself (and Sometimes Other People): Spiritual*

Advice for Modern Relationships. She leads workshops and retreats on finding the soul-voice within. She has a Master's of Theological Studies from Harvard Divinity School and a Master's of Divinity from Union Theological Seminary. She lives with her young son and his imaginary goose, Goldie.

Website: www.megganwatterson.com

≈

Mike Dooley is a former PriceWaterhouseCoopers international tax consultant, turned entrepreneur, who's founded a philosophical Adventurers Club on the Internet that's now home to over 700,000 members from over 185 countries. His inspirational books emphasizing spiritual accountability have been published in 25 languages, and he was one of the featured teachers in the international phenomenon, *The Secret.* Today Mike is perhaps best known for his free Notes from the Universe e-mailings and his *New York Times* bestsellers *Infinite Possibilities: The Art of Living Your Dreams* and *Leveraging the Universe: 7 Steps to Engaging Life's Magic.* Mike lives what he teaches, traveling internationally speaking on life, dreams, and happiness.

Find out more at tut.com.

≈

Mona Lisa Schulz, M.D., Ph.D., is one of those rare people who can cross the borders of science, medicine, and mysticism. She is a practicing neuropsychiatrist and an associate professor of psychiatry at the University of Vermont College of Medicine. She has been a medical intuitive for 25 years. Dr. Mona Lisa has published several books, including *All Is Well* with Louise Hay, *The Intuitive Advisor, The New Feminine Brain,* and *Awakening Intuition.* She lives between Yarmouth, Maine, and Franklin, Tennessee, with her four cats and assorted wildlife.

Website: www.DrMonaLisa.com

≈

Nick Ortner is CEO of The Tapping Solution, LLC, a company with a mission to bring simple, effective, natural healing into the mainstream through Emotional Freedom Techniques (EFT) or "tapping." He is the author of the *New York Times* best-selling book, *The Tapping Solution: A Revolutionary System for Stress-Free Living,* and the creator and producer of the breakthrough documentary film *The Tapping Solution,* which follows ten people who used tapping to overcome tremendous challenges, including 30 years of chronic back pain, fibromyalgia, insomnia, devastating grief, and more. Both Nick's book and film document real and extraordinary results that have inspired tens of thousands to follow suit by successfully applying tapping to their lives. Nick is the producer of the Tapping World Summit, a free, worldwide online event that just celebrated its fifth successful season and has been attended by over 1,000,000 people (www.tappingworldsummit.com).

Follow Nick on Twitter @NickOrtner and see him on Facebook at www.facebook.com/NOrtner.

Website: www.TheTappingSolution.com

Noah St. John is a keynote speaker and author of ten books, including his Hay House bestseller *AFFORMATIONS®: The Miracle of Positive Self-Talk.* Noah is famous for helping busy people enjoy emotional and financial freedom. His sought-after advice is known as the "secret sauce" in personal and business growth. As the leading authority on how to boost performance and profits, Noah delivers live events and online courses that have been called "the only training that fixes every other training!" He also appears frequently in the news media worldwide, including ABC, NBC, CBS, Fox, the Hallmark Channel, National Public Radio, *Parade, Woman's Day, Chicago Sun-Times,* Forbes.com, and The Huffington Post. You can get Noah's new book, *Mastering the Inner Game of Success,* for free at www.NoahStJohn.com.

Pam Grout is the author of 18 books, including the #1 *New York Times* bestseller *E-Squared: Nine Do-It-Yourself Energy Experiments That Prove Your Thoughts Create Your Reality.* She is also the author of three plays, a television series, and two iPhone apps. She writes for *People* magazine, CNN, *Men's Journal,* The Huffington Post, and her travel blog, www.georgeclooneyslepthere.com.

Find out more about Pam and her out-of-the-box take on life on her website: www.pamgrout.com.

≈

Sandra Anne Taylor is the *New York Times* best-selling author of *Quantum Success; Secrets of Attraction;* and her most recent, *Your Quantum Breakthrough Code,* which offers an amazingly easy, yet profoundly powerful, tool for change. Sandra is known for her inspiring processes and life-changing techniques incorporating consciousness, karma, and energy in personal transformation. Her beautiful deck of *Energy Oracle Cards* helps you identify present patterns and predict future results. *The Hidden Power of Your Past Lives* (book-with-CD) helps you eradicate past-life blocks. Sandra's titles are available in 27 languages across the globe, and she can be heard on Mondays at HayHouseRadio.com.

Websites: www.SandraTaylor.net and www.Facebook.com /SandraAnneTaylor

≈

Sonia Choquette is a world-renowned author, storyteller, vibrational healer, and six-sensory spiritual teacher in international demand for her guidance, wisdom, and capacity to heal the soul. She is the author of the *New York Times* bestseller *The Answer Is Simple . . . ,* among other books; as well as numerous audio programs and card decks. Sonia was educated at the University of Denver and the Sorbonne in Paris, and holds a Ph.D. in metaphysics from the American Institute of Holistic Theology. She presently resides in Paris.

Website: www.soniachoquette.com

≈

ABOUT THE AUTHOR

Gerry Gavin is a speaker, life coach, medium, and host of a very popular weekly radio program on www.HayHouseRadio.com, which has a loyal international following. He is the creator of the very successful Angels & Shamans workshop, which puts participants in direct connection with their angels and guides. He channels the angel Margaret, who conveys life-changing, down-to-earth angelic advice, at public appearances, on radio programs, and in private readings. He also specializes in shamanic healing practices that help individuals to reclaim their power, health, and even lost pieces of their soul through a process called soul retrieval. His work is a combination of modern therapeutic techniques and ancient healing practices that listen to the body, mind, and spirit to help clients reach their fullest potential. Gerry lives on a small horse farm in New Jersey.

Website: www.gerrygavin.com

NOTES

NOTES

Hay House Titles of Related Interest

YOU CAN HEAL YOUR LIFE, the movie, starring Louise Hay & Friends
(available as a 1-DVD program and an expanded 2-DVD set)
Watch the trailer at: www.LouiseHayMovie.com

THE SHIFT, the movie,
starring Dr. Wayne W. Dyer
(available as a 1-DVD program and an expanded 2-DVD set)
Watch the trailer at: www.DyerMovie.com

❧

Dying to Be Me: My Journey from Cancer, to Near Death, to True Healing,
by Anita Moorjani

Messages from Spirit: The Extraordinary Power of Oracles, Omens, and Signs,
by Colette Baron-Reid

The Tapping Solution: A Revolutionary System for Stress-Free Living,
by Nick Ortner

*Through the Eyes Of Another: A Medium's Guide to Creating Heaven on Earth
by Encountering Your Life Review Now,* by Karen Noé

The Top Ten Things Dead People Want to Tell YOU, by Mike Dooley

❧

All of the above are available at your local bookstore,
or may be ordered by visiting:

Hay House USA: www.hayhouse.com®
Hay House Australia: www.hayhouse.com.au
Hay House UK: www.hayhouse.co.uk
Hay House South Africa: www.hayhouse.co.za
Hay House India: www.hayhouse.co.in

We hope you enjoyed this Hay House book. If you'd like to receive our online catalog featuring additional information on Hay House books and products, or if you'd like to find out more about the Hay Foundation, please contact:

Hay House, Inc., P.O. Box 5100, Carlsbad, CA 92018-5100
(760) 431-7695 or (800) 654-5126
(760) 431-6948 (fax) or (800) 650-5115 (fax)
www.hayhouse.com® • www.hayfoundation.org

≈

Published and distributed in Australia by: Hay House Australia Pty. Ltd., 18/36 Ralph St., Alexandria NSW 2015 • *Phone:* 612-9669-4299 • *Fax:* 612-9669-4144 www.hayhouse.com.au

Published and distributed in the United Kingdom by: Hay House UK, Ltd., Astley House, 33 Notting Hill Gate, London W11 3JQ • *Phone:* 44-20-3675-2450 *Fax:* 44-20-3675-2451 • www.hayhouse.co.uk

Published and distributed in the Republic of South Africa by: Hay House SA (Pty), Ltd., P.O. Box 990, Witkoppen 2068 • info@hayhouse.co.za • www.hayhouse.co.za

Published in India by: Hay House Publishers India, Muskaan Complex, Plot No. 3, B-2, Vasant Kunj, New Delhi 110 070 • *Phone:* 91-11-4176-1620 *Fax:* 91-11-4176-1630 • www.hayhouse.co.in

Distributed in Canada by: Raincoast Books, 2440 Viking Way, Richmond, B.C. V6V 1N2 • *Phone:* 1-800-663-5714 • *Fax:* 1-800-565-3770 • www.raincoast.com

≈

Take Your Soul on a Vacation

Visit www.HealYourLife.com® to regroup, recharge, and reconnect with your own magnificence. Featuring blogs, mind-body-spirit news, and life-changing wisdom from Louise Hay and friends.

Visit www.HealYourLife.com today!

Free e-newsletters
from Hay House, the Ultimate Resource for Inspiration

Be the first to know about Hay House's dollar deals, free downloads, special offers, affirmation cards, giveaways, contests, and more!

Get exclusive excerpts from our latest releases and videos from *Hay House Present Moments*.

Enjoy uplifting personal stories, how-to articles, and healing advice, along with videos and empowering quotes, within *Heal Your Life*.

Have an inspirational story to tell and a passion for writing? Sharpen your writing skills with insider tips from *Your Writing Life*.

Sign Up Now!

Get inspired, educate yourself, get a complimentary gift, and share the wisdom!

http://www.hayhouse.com/newsletters.php

Visit www.hayhouse.com to sign up today!

HealYourLife.com ♥